IT TAKES SO LITTLE

TO BE *Above Average*

Florence Littauer

HARVEST HOUSE PUBLISHERS
Eugene, Oregon 97402

Other books by Florence Littauer

After Every Wedding Comes a Marriage
Blow Away the Black Clouds
Pursuit of Happiness
Personality Plus
Shades of Beauty

Unless otherwise noted all Scripture verses are taken from the King James Version.

IT TAKES SO LITTLE TO BE ABOVE AVERAGE

Copyright © 1983 by Harvest House Publishers
Eugene, Oregon 97402

Third printing, March 1984
Library of Congress Catalog Card Number 83-80120
ISBN 0-89081-376-0

Printed in the United States of America.

CONTENTS

FOREWORD

In the early '70s women were crying "equality" and getting into the job market with demands they had never voiced before. Out of necessity, I found myself talking to the vice-president of Farmers Insurance Group about becoming an agent. "We don't want women," he said, "but by law, I must give you a chance. If you think you can do a man's job and meet the same requirements, we'll give you the opportunity."

I studied hard, worked late, passed my licensing examination, and met the prerequisites to become a full-line insurance agent. I set my goals for the first year and finished them in nine months. I had proved myself and was no longer on probation.

The production charts showed that our region, which covered a six-state area, had 700 men that were doing an "average job," and that out of that number some were making the "Top Twenty" list. I wanted to make the "Top Twenty" list so I created the motto, IT TAKES SO LITTLE TO BE ABOVE AVERAGE.

I went on to achieve my goal as one of the "Top Twenty" agents and won awards, trips, and walls of plaques. My ultimate accomplishment was receiving the "Distinguished Salesman Award," given to only 33 people in the State of Colorado each year in all sales fields. I attended a banquet at the Hilton Ballroom and was presented my trophy by the mayor of Denver. I was no longer average.

A few years later, the Lord led me to sell my successful agency and pursue the calling of Christian writer and speaker. A dear friend had challenged me, saying I had much to share and I had a burning desire to help hurting women.

I had a purpose but no plan, desire but no delivery, ideas but no image.

After struggling with the fact that I no longer had a professional handle, that my goals were stymied by lack of training, God sent Florence into my life. Two weeks later I flew to Dallas for her sixth Christian Leaders and Speakers Seminar (C.L.A.S.S.). I knew this was what I had been searching for. That week I observed an ABOVE AVERAGE woman challenge, motivate, and love 86 women into *their* being ABOVE AVERAGE.

She taught me to organize my ideas and helped me to set a goal in anything I said or wrote. Because the rewards in the professional world were empty, I had left my career. I *pursued* what I felt to be God's will for my life, and he has given me a *purpose* and sent *people* such as Florence to challenge, encourage, and believe in me.

I thank God for Florence as I pursue excellence by following her example. She has proven that in the Christian world it is acceptable to strive, achieve and be ABOVE AVERAGE to God's glory.

You will be challenged in reading this book as you learn:

It Takes So Little To Be Above Average!

Francine Jackson

Evergreen, Colorado

A

It Takes So Little
To Feel Above Average

1

Pursue Excellence

Some women want to run everything they can get their hands on and others would rather die than become involved with leadership. Whichever type you are, the day may come when this kind of responsibility falls upon you and you find yourself perilously unprepared. Those who are fearful sometimes become chairman by a process of elimination and then whimper their way through the year. Even those who love to be up front sometimes hope to run the whole church off the top of their heads.

I went one night to a women's "group meeting" where the nominating chairman stood up and said, "We didn't have time to meet and so what I thought would be fun would be if we went right around the room and each one of you say why you *couldn't* be next year's chairman. The one with the worst excuse will be it."

It was my first meeting and when it got to me, I stated, "I will only be in town for two of the eight meetings." The lady next to me sniffled into her hankie as she cried, "My husband's an atheist and he'd be furious if he found out I was chairman of any church committee." Others had extremely creative and colorful excuses, and when the vote was taken the weepy lady and I tied. I pointed out to them how important it is to have a chairman who can be at the meetings and they released me. Mrs. Weepy became Leader by Default and they promised her no one would ever tell her husband she had won.

I left as quickly as I could, dumbfounded at their total lack of parliamentary procedures and grateful the mantle of leadership had been dropped on someone else.

If you were that lady where would you turn for help? There is no quick school for instant presidents, but there are some simple steps that can make you ABOVE AVERAGE. It takes so little.

Nobody *wants* to be average. We don't seek to be ordinary, dull, usual, run-of-the-mill! We'd rather be unique, inspiring, significant, ABOVE AVERAGE.

Then why do so many of us trudge down the middle lane of life? Why do we wander through a whole year, rip off the month of December, and wonder what it's all been worth? Why is there always a shortage of leadership in any organization? Or as *Newsweek* asked on its cover, "Where have all the heroes gone?"[1]

During the last thirty years of relative affluence, we haven't had to be heroes. We have been able to progress while standing still. We've been able to advance while remaining average. Mediocrity has become accepted as the norm and people who have tried to excel in any endeavor have been looked upon as odd or pushy. Even the church has been satisfied to accept average as good enough and has labeled the achiever as worldly. Jack Taylor, an ABOVE AVERAGE evangelist and author, says, "Our adversary would divide us by leading us to suppose that aspirations to succeed and humility were enemies; that the Holy Spirit deplores personal motivation; and that positive thinking is an enemy of total commitment."[2]

Don't you sometimes long for a *real* leader, for a hero who wants to right wrongs, for a heroine who is pure and virtuous? The Bible still asks, "Who can find a virtuous woman? for her price is far above rubies."[3] Yes, who *can* find a virtuous woman, one who is truly ABOVE AVERAGE?

The late TV anchorwoman, Jessica Savitch, received an honorary degree from Columbia College in Columbia, S.C., in June, 1983. In challenging the graduates she said:

> As a reporter, I have had a chance to observe people
> at the top of just about every field. And it makes no
> difference if they are male or female, black or white,
> old or young, the people I observed succeeding are
> those who have been taught or who teach themselves
> to strive for excellence. The pleasure comes from

knowing you have done a job the best way you know how. It seems to me, however, in our modern society that there is very little done these days in pursuit of excellence. But whatever there is, it stands out for its rarity.[4]

Wouldn't you like to be a rarity, far above rubies? There is such a *need* for leadership today, so many cries for direction. We need women who are willing to say, "Here am I, use me." We need older women to teach the young. We *need*:

- women who are examples for others to follow
- women who are willing to take a chance
- women who will encourage others
- women who aren't touchy or petty
- women who can think beyond the moment
- women who have the attitude and bearing of a leader
- women who try to look their best
- women who can call a meeting to order
- women who will open their homes
- women who have compassion for those in trouble
- women who are ready to pursue excellence

There are so few virtuous women around, so few pursuing excellence in either the world or the average church. Are you willing to read these pages, spend some time on introspection and reflective thinking, set some new goals?

Because the average of the past has been below average, it is easy for us in the present to aim to be ABOVE AVERAGE in the future.

Let's stand out as a rarity and reach for a crown of rubies.

It Takes So Little To Be ABOVE AVERAGE.

2

Take Aim

We can easily see the demand there is for competent women to minister to women in need, but how are they going to be trained and who is going to train them.

I never cease to be amazed that God has a specific plan for each one of our lives and that He knows the beginning from the end. I marvel as I look back over a half-century of experience and see how God has woven my life together and put me in a place of ministry far different from *my* original plans.

He gave me a British father who instilled in me a love for words and a desire to speak clearly.

He gave me a sensitive mother, a violin and cello teacher, who sent me to elocution lessons because I had "no musical talent."

He allowed me to receive a scholarship to college where I steeped myself in English literature, apprenticed as a director of musical comedies, and won the title of Best Female Speaker in New England Colleges.

He gave me the ability to teach English and speech on the high school and college level, to direct little theatre productions, and to do fashion commentating for Macy's in New York.

He allowed me to be brought to my knees by the births of two hopelessly brain-damaged sons and gave me a genuine compassion for people with problems.

He gave me victory over depression and put me in leadership positions from State Budget Chairman of the League of Women

Voters in Connecticut to District Public Speaking Chairman for the Federated Women's Clubs of America.

He allowed my husband Fred and me to pull our marriage together and then teach others "how to." He gave me a ministry of motivating, consoling and inspiring women, and now He has pulled it all together so that I can show others how to give hope to a troubled world.

As I was on a cross-country airplane in the fall of 1980, I read a *Vogue* article that said the '80s would be the "Decade of the Active Woman." It predicted that women would be seeking training as never before in whatever courses were available. I wondered what was available, and who was going to teach it. When I returned home I looked in the *Los Angeles Times* Calendar section[1] and was amazed at the variety of events planned for that week. Courses were open to the public on:

Psychological Analysis of Zen Meditation
Beginning a New Life Through Simple Relaxation
Altruistic Activism: Best Exercise for Good Health
Hypnosis: The Key to Your Subconscious Mind

Was *Vogue*'s prediction correct? Were people seeking seminars of self-help? The answer came clearly two years later when the *Times* printed a major article, "Americans Take a Long Look Inward."

According to social researchers, 80% of America's adult population is now actively engaged in seeking self-fulfillment. For better or worse, the so-called human potential movement has grown up to become a staple of the culture.[2]

These "crash courses in personal growth" have crashed upon us as waves. So many are coming so fast that one Los Angeles lady has installed a seven-terminal computer system to keep track of the new seminars each week. She publishes a directory of seminars and plans "to start seminars of her own—including seminars for people who want to give seminars."[3]

Suddenly we have realized we've been treading water and we want to catch the next wave to success. We want to be ABOVE AVERAGE.

If it's true that 80% of the American adult population is seeking self-fulfillment, that figure has to include much of the Christian community. Where are these courses? What are they teaching? Who is doing the instruction?

These questions led me to a sobering thought. These courses are *in* the world and *of* the world and they are taught by people smart enough to seize an opportunity when they see one. While the church is discussing the color of the new choir robes, its members are running off to worldly courses in hope of finding themselves and becoming relevant.

We can't ignore the "Decade of the Active Woman"; we must provide the leadership for such a time as this. With this need in mind, I invited forty Christian women to attend a speakers training seminar in my hometown of Redlands, California in February of 1981. These were all women who had the potential for influential leadership and who only needed the tools and the motivation. Among those who attended were four Hollywood personalities who were ready to learn how to lead for the Lord. Rhonda Fleming, an exquisitely elegant lady, was motivated to express her faith openly. Since then she has been on the 700 Club twice, has given her testimony to 1000 women in Minneapolis, and has related her story in *Guideposts*. Bonnie Green, former showgirl, and husband Johnny Green, the composer and conductor, have both appeared on the 700 Club and have a ministry with couples in Beverly Hills. Joanne Dru is now sharing her testimony with others and Jeanne Cagney has already inspired and challenged the audience at the Southern California Women's Retreat.

God has already *given* these women talent, charm, and personality. He had allowed each one to go through trials and traumas that had brought them to their knees. They had the message of hope for discouraged women. All they needed were the tools, the know-how to move out of the wings and onto the stage of life.

As I observed the remarkable changes in the women during fours days of training and the ministries God impressed upon them as they became equipped, I knew I had to do my part to fill the leadership gap in the Christian community. I knew the Lord wanted to use me to lift the levels of Christian communications. With my husband's encouragement and support, I founded C.L.A.S.S.—Christian Leaders and Speakers Seminars. In the last two years the Lord has used this instrument to give tools and motivation to over 1000 women across the country. He has provided me with a staff of dedicated women who want to teach others to "Say it with C.L.A.S.S." Some of us plant, some of us water, and God gives the increase.

What about you? Are you ready for God's exciting plan for your life?

It may not take a lot to be ABOVE AVERAGE, but it does take something. It takes desire. Do you care enough to try? It takes a goal. Do you wish to aim high? You've perhaps heard of the airline pilot who announced over the loudspeaker. "I have bad news and good news. The bad news is we're lost and don't know where we're going. The good news is we're making very good time." This simple story represents many of our lives. We're lost, we don't know where we're going, but we're rushing on to get there.

Dr. E.V. Hill, the dynamic black evangelist, recently challenged a group of leaders at the First Baptist Church in Dallas to "report for duty." He told us that there is a wide gate and a broad way that leads to destruction and many there are that go down it. But straight is the gate and narrow the way which leads to life—"...and few there be that find it."[4] He stated, "It takes no brains to find the broad way. You just waddle out one day and you're on it. But if you want to find the narrow way you've got to look for it. You've got to aim for it—and few there be that find it."

There are so many articles and books on motivation that it seems too obvious to mention the importance of setting goals, to find the "narrow way." We all know that without a vision the people perish and that we are to do all things cheerfully as unto the Lord; but sometimes the vision is fuzzy and our cheery has turned to dreary.

While we all accept that our first human priority is to care for our families, we should open our minds to the fact that our whole life is a preparation for ministry. For you young women who are at home with the children, don't let your mind wander out to pasture. Keep alert, keep reading, keep thinking. Know that God will give you a ministry when He feels you are ready. Don't wait until you can see the handwriting on the wall; use every available mental moment to prepare *today* for God's call *tomorrow*.

One summer when I was teaching drama at Camp Trebor, the archery instructor quit. The director asked if anyone could teach the class. No one volunteered even though additional wages sweetened the proposition. I did a quick mental review of my college archery class and raised my hand. Even though I had little athletic ability, I remembered the basic principles of the sport and I lined the young girls up in the field with their bows and arrows. At first we had no target; the girls had to get the arrow moving and learn the basic skills. When they could simply send the shaft sailing somewhere, we set up a target. Up until then they were playing games, but they didn't have a goal. It's hard to hit the target when you don't have one. As each girl focused in, she narrowed her aim until she found the target. Some hit the straw around the edge, some scored, and a few found the bull's-eye.

Some of us don't want to practice or prepare until the final target is right before us and we can see the bull's-eye, and yet God often does not reveal His ultimate plan until He sees that we are ready. He doesn't reach down for the idle mind, the lazy body, or the empty spirit. He wants someone who's preparing for the future even when she can't see the target.

Abraham Lincoln was an unlikely candidate for any political office, let alone the presidency of the United States. He was homely, plain, and simple. He did not possess the magnetism or charisma we all want in a leader. Even though he did not look or act like a leader, he prepared for leadership and said, "I'll study and get ready, and then maybe my chance will come."

As I train leaders in C.L.A.S.S., I find a few who don't want to "waste time" aiming to be ABOVE AVERAGE in case they never get called on to lead, but would God waste a prepared person? Especially one who prepared on faith not knowing the exact goal?

Nina Jean Obel, a lovely Dallas lady with an exceptional home, innate class and breeding, and elegant designer clothes, came to one of our leadership seminars. She took the training not expecting to use it, but wanting to experience all life had to offer. In the eyes of the world she had arrived and she could rest on her silk damask couch and watch the swans sail by her window. But Nina Jean wanted to be available for the Lord's call whatever that might be and she came to study. Barbara Bueler was her group leader and Nina Jean said to her, "I don't know why I'm doing this because I'm really very shy and I don't like to stand up in front of anyone, but I want to be ready."

One morning as Nina Jean sat in a meeting of the Dallas chapter of the Great Commission Prayer Crusade, the ladies were discussing the need to train speakers to meet the demands they had for prayer workshops. No one seemed to know anyone with ability in leadership training and as the vacuum became more apparent, Nina Jean wondered, was this the place God had in mind for her?

Quietly she raised her hand and told them she had been to C.L.A.S.S. Within minutes Nina Jean became the leader of all those who were willing to receive instruction. As she told me this story she said in amazement, "I can't believe I'm doing this, but I seemed to be the only one who was ready."

Today there are so many opportunites for women who are ready. There are so many groups desperate for leaders, so many lonely people craving for attention, so many depressed souls waiting for uplifting counsel. Are you ready?

A 96-year-old lady was a faithful attendant at my women's club Bible studies. She came with her lessons prepared and knew all the answers. One day a tactless member asked her, "Why do you work so hard on these lessons when you're so old and it doesn't matter?"

Little Bess Elkins looked up and said confidently, "I'm cramming for my finals."

It's never too late to get ready for our finals. Narrow is the way which leads to life and few there be that find it. It takes so little to be ABOVE AVERAGE, but it does take a desire to learn and it does take preparation so when the great target appears we'll be able to hit the bull's-eye.

In an elegant ad for the sporty and expensive Alfa Romeo, the headline states, "Now that you've got your act together, take it on the road." I read the copy which tells me I can have a car tailored to fit me so well, "You don't just drive it. You practically wear it."

As I dreamed over this thought, I realized how many of us have gone out on the road before "we got our act together."

How about you? Let's make the effort to come in from the highways and byways of life and spend some time in soul-searching and self-improvement. Then when the simple steps and spiritual supplements give you new strength, you'll have your act together and you'll be able to take it on the road, wherever God leads.

It Takes So Little To Be ABOVE AVERAGE.

3

Move Up to Zero

Some people feel they'll never get their act together, that they'll never take it on the road. How about you? Do you think you're below average? Have you grown up somehow feeling insecure? Do you have a low self-image? Do other people always seem smarter or better looking?

As Christians we don't want a worldly focus on ourselves, yet it is foolish to be held down by an inferiority complex that keeps us from encouraging others. Many of us feel that since Paul said, "In me is no good thing," we are to live in a constant state of self-flagellation and if anyone compliments us we should instantly deny the praise and negate any uplifting thought. In David Seamands book, *Healing for Damaged Emotions*, he corrects the faulty theology that a self-belittling attitude is pleasing to God. He says this precept

> ...Is not true Christian humility and runs counter to some very basic teachings of the Christian faith. The great commandment is that you love God with all your being. The second commandment is an extension of the first—that you love your neighbor as you love yourself. We do not have two commandments here, but three: to love God, to love yourself, and to love others. I put *self* second, because Jesus plainly made a proper self-love the basis of a proper love for a

neighbor. The term *self-love* has a wrong connotation for some people. Whether you call it self-esteem or self-worth, it is plainly the foundation of Christian love for others. And this is the opposite of what many Christians believe.[1]

When we ask Jesus Christ into our hearts He promises to come in and give us abundant lives. He adopts us into His family, we become just a little lower than the angels, we are His royal priesthood, we are the temple of His Holy Spirit and we know when He comes again we will be like Him. We are children of the King and yet so few of us lay hold of that truth. It's difficult to be ABOVE AVERAGE when our self-worth isn't yet up to zero.

One lady wrote me after our Ft. Worth C.L.A.S.S. and poured out her heart. "Over the years when I would attend a funeral I would wonder what the preacher would have good to say about me. I had let my self-image be pretty low a lot of the time."

Maureen Jordan came to our C.L.A.S.S. at the Crystal Cathedral in Southern California and confessed a lifetime of traumas that had left her with an extremely low picture of herself. As the staff ministered to her, she began to look at herself in a new light, unfolding in a radiant manner. Later she wrote:

> C.L.A.S.S. meant so much to me. It was a turning point, a life-changing experience. You have given me HOPE that I can someday share my story in such a way that others may know Jesus Christ and His unconditional love for us all. We don't hear as much of how He restores our broken self-image when we come to Him as I would like. So maybe someday soon I'll be one of his healed helpers. I have confidence that God shall complete and perfect an emotional healing for me.

Are you a little insecure or self-conscious? Are you not quite up to zero? Let's take a self-image inventory. On the next page is a list of physical, mental, and spiritual areas in your life about which you have a ready-made opinion.

1. Read each item and then put down the first descriptive word that comes to your mind. For example, I would write: Hair, straight; Looks, plain; Intellect, smart. Do only this first column now.

SELF-IMAGE

What is it? The opinion and value you place on yourself, the reflection of your inner person.

What is the origin? Parents, friends, employers, mates, children, self.

Is self-image correct? Take this self-analysis.

	Descriptive Word	Origin of Opinion
Looks		
Hair		
Eyes		
Weight & shape		
Posture & bearing		
Clothes		
Sense of style & color		
Self-confidence		
Personality		
Intellect		
Ability to converse		
Knowing current events		
Leadership skills		
Spiritual dedication		
Bible knowledge		
Compassion for others		

2. After you have written words of self-evaluation, go back and count how many are positive and how many are negative. My straight hair and plain looks would both be negatives and my smart mind would be a plus. If you have more negatives than positives, you obviously do not have a healthy self-image. But we won't leave the matter there. Let's look at the next column.

3. Read each item and descriptive word again. Think back as far as you can to when you first got that opinion of yourself. Who first gave you that idea? What incident caused you to draw this conclusion of yourself?

I remember an aunt who said to my mother, "Don't worry about Florence being so plain; they all improve as they grow up." When I think back, I know how hurt I was in first grade when I tried out for the part of the Rose or even the Lily and was chosen as the Cowslip. My whole role was to walk heavy-footed across the stage and then fall down in a heap. As I picked myself up, everyone laughed because I had ripped my crepe paper petals off in the fall. I was so embarrassed and realized I had a "dumb part" because I wasn't pretty. Each spring our church had a May Day celebration and lovely little girls were chosen to dance delicately around a maypole weaving streamers in and out. When I volunteered, they asked me to sit on the box in order to hold the maypole steady. At Christmas I wanted to be Mary, but I didn't try out when the Sunday school teacher said, "Only the pretty girls should come." In high school I wanted a lead in the senior class play, *The Fighting Littles*. The all-American beauties got the parts and I had a few lines as Cuckoo, the dingbat.

As you read over the negatives about yourself, think about where you first got these thoughts. Jot down the occasion or the person who planted this concept in your mind.

Now do the same with the positives. I remember so many times when I'd be standing up next to my little brother Jim and people would say to my mother, "Isn't Jim adorable with his curls!" Then they'd look at me and sigh, "She must be smart." I decided very early in life that I had better get smart. It seemed to be my only asset so I studied hard. In high school I got on the honor roll, won a scholarship to college, carried three full majors, stayed on the dean's list, and graduated with honors in speech. At least I was smart!

As I have gone over this chart with women in seminars, I have learned how consistently the basis for our self-image comes from people and events in our childhood. Perhaps it was a teacher who said, "Why aren't you smart like your sister?"; a father who shouted, "You trip over everything!"; a mother who sighed, "We've done the best we can with her."; a stranger who patted you on the head and said, "You're cute for a fat girl."

Where did our poor self-image come from? Now, what are we going to do with the negative results? It's not enough to *face* the facts that we have some low opinions of ourselves or even to *trace* their origins. We now have to work to *erase* these attitudes. We don't need to carry the burden of thoughtless people from long ago and far away on our backs any longer. By now some of you may have had your eyes opened. You know why you haven't felt secure within yourself. Just this revelation is often a relief.

Does this negative feeling have any sound foundation at this point in my life? Am I dragging a dead horse around the block? Do I need to be worried about straight hair anymore? No. We have permanents, curling irons, and hot rollers at our disposal and, for a change or cover-up, there are wigs, and hairpieces. There is hardly a woman alive who can't have curly hair today.

Am I still that plain little girl who lived in three rooms behind the grocery store? Am I still in Work Progress Administration dresses that come in three pastel shades? Yes, inside I am. I'm still waiting to play the role of the queen, still wanting to win a beauty contest, still shocked when someone calls me elegant. Do you see how early impressions hang on even when there is conflicting evidence?

Let's get rid of these ridiculous carry-overs today. Let's look at them for what they are: ancient history that we have allowed to drag us down far too long. Go over your list and draw a line right through each negative word that is *not valid* anymore. You aren't fat or dumb. You don't have beady eyes or a bad complexion.

Paul tells us in Philippians 3:13-14 (RSV), "One thing I do, forgetting what lies behind and straining forward to what lies ahead, I press on towards the goal for the prize of the upward call of God in Christ Jesus." Cross off your list and erase those unnecessary burdens. Don't let an old aunt who is now dead ruin your self-image. Don't let a third-grade teacher have control over you when you're thirty years of age. Don't let a casual comment tossed lightly years ago hang heavily upon you today.

Anne Thornton came to our first C.L.A.S.S. and filled out this self-image chart. Later she told me this time of introspection had opened up her eyes to some previously unexplained hang-ups. She saw the background reasons for some of her insecurities and realized how ridiculous it was that criticism heard in her childhood was still influencing her opinion of herself today. As she prayerfully worked to overcome these insidious relics of the past, she was able to free her mind from the quiet brooding that had been a resident negative all her life. As she examined and released these old evaluations, she was able to apply these same steps to helping other women in her Bibly study class. Her leadership skills improved as she was able to accept herself as God had made her, not as other people had influenced her to believe.

The next time someone compliments you on one of your touchy areas, thank the person instantly and thank the Lord for this reinforcement and this healing of your own esteem. Now ask the next question.

Is this negative feeling actually a valid problem in my life? If it is, what am I going to do about it?

Francine Jackson, one of our C.L.A.S.S. staff, told me how as a child she was laughed at because she "ran funny." Later people called her gawky and gangly. She was the tallest girl in her high school class and some said her neck was too long. She tried to pull her head down into her shoulders and she slumped over when she walked, but she still knew people were staring at her and whispering about her. Her teeth weren't even, so she tried not to smile. Do you see how much effort was going into cover-up activity? "I felt like a turtle," Francine said. "I wanted to pull my head, neck, and limbs inside a shell and hide."

What do you do when you examine yourself and find these evaluations to be at least partly true? Francine began to keep a journal of her feelings. "Lord, I feel awkward and I want to be graceful. What should I do?" As she put her thoughts on paper, she began to deal with them first in her heart and then in her actions. She decided to stand up straight and be stately. She held her head up high and her long neck became regal. She bought clothes with collars that stood up and framed her neck, not choked it off. She began to walk with confidence. As she worked prayerfully and humanly on her shortcomings, people's comments changed. "You have lovely long legs." "What a graceful neck!" "Beautiful posture."

As Francine's self-confidence improved she dared take on her other problem, and at thirty-seven years of age she had braces put on her teeth. Those have since been taken off, revealing an even, beautiful smile.

What do you do if you think of yourself as fat and you are? What do you do if you feel you dress poorly and you do? What if your teenager says your glasses frames are old-fashioned and they are? What if your friends get mad because you're always late, and you are? What if your husband says you don't know what's going on in the world and you don't?

Do you see how easy it is to come up with answers to these hypothetical questions? But what are you going to do about the real ones?

After listening to my tape on "Marriage Preservation," Liz Page realized her knowledge of the news was limited. She decided to take action and she wrote me:

> I made a date with my husband to watch the ten o'clock
> news. A feminine bathrobe, two glasses of cider, and
> a willingness to discuss the news (as I *used* to) made
> for a happy husband. Thanks for the nudge!

We all need to be nudged into action in some area of our lives. Let's review our concerns and some possible cures. You've written down quick descriptive words about yourself. You've counted up the negatives and you've looked back in your life to see where you first got these ideas. You've asked yourself whether there is any validity in these opinions in the light of today. When you thought about these attitudes, you realized how ridiculous they were and you crossed them right off the page and prayed them right out of your mind.

Now look at the leftovers, problems that still need solutions. List them on the lines below. What kind of action should you take? Do you need to lose weight? Update your hair, makeup, glasses frames? Listen to the news and read a few books? Get yourself on a schedule? Think over these areas where you have a negative self-image and then plan some actions you can take about them. It's so easy to sit around in the ashes of self-pity waiting for a fairy godmother to transform us, but let's not allow our insecurities to become cover-ups for laziness or excuses for inaction. You do the possible and let God do the impossible.

Concerns	Action
_____ _____	_____ _____
_____ _____	_____ _____
_____ _____	_____ _____
_____ _____	_____ _____

This action list becomes your new set of goals. Are there some things left that you can't do much about at the moment? Ones that need *more space*—a special area for you to read or study; a closet for off-season clothes; a playroom for the children; *more money*—redecorating the living room; updating your wardrobe; getting your teeth straightened; *more time*—doing some home baking; altering your clothes; enrolling in a college course; writing the great American novel?

Write down these concerns, hopes and dreams, giving yourself some suggestions on what future action you could take. This list becomes your long-range goals.

Concerns	Future Action
_____ _____	_____ _____
_____ _____	_____ _____
_____ _____	_____ _____
_____ _____	_____ _____

What negatives are still on your list? Are there some things left that, short of plastic surgery or a new brain, you can't do anything

about? You have short legs, you can't write poetry, or you look
just like your least favorite aunt? Write down these thoughts that
have troubled you.

Concerns			Acceptance	
————	————		————	————
————	————		————	————
————	————		————	————
————	————		————	————

Read them objectively and laugh at how petty these problems
really are. Ask the Lord to help you accept yourself as you are,
knowing that not one of us is perfect and so many others are in
extremely trying situations.

At our C.L.A.S.S. in Tampa we had a beautiful lady attend in
a wheelchair. She had cancer and her leg had been amputated
to the hip. She had an artificial limb which was extremely uncomfortable and she was in constant pain. In spite of this, she
stood up when it was her turn to introduce herself and she smiled
bravely as tears came down her cheeks. She participated in each
activity and was gracious to everyone who spoke with her. By
the end of the three days together the other women realized how
trivial many of their problems were. You could not complain that
God didn't give you two lovely legs when you observed the
strength of a lady who only had one.

Review the concerns you wrote down. Do they really matter?
As you check off God's acceptance of you, begin to accept yourself
as you are.

So many women come to me with weight problems that have
become such burdens to them that the concerns are usurping control over their actions and personalities. Some have supposedly
tried every diet in the world and can't lose an ounce. They've
bought every diet book and gone to every health seminar and
nothing has helped. I know one girl who has three lifetime
memberships in health clubs and only has "guilt over not going"
as her result. Many women talk endlessly about their diets and
defeats, making themselves not only overweight but boring.

What do you do if you can't overcome a problem and you have sincerely tried? You accept the situation and say, "Dear Lord, You know I don't want to be this way. I have tried to eliminate this area of my life and it's still here. Help me to accept myself as I am and not ruin my whole life over one problem. I know You made me and love me and don't want me harping on this subject any longer. When You are ready, lead me to victory."

A lovely young girl came up to me recently and told me she had listened to me speak when I used Philippians 4:11, "...I have learned, in whatsoever state I am, therewith to be content." I had asked the audience to think of things that they were upset over and not content about. She realized she was set on having a baby and after eight years of marriage could not get pregnant, regardless of tests, vitamins, exercise, minor surgery, prayer.

That day, at my suggestion, she gave up her obsession over having a baby and asked the Lord to make her content without being a mother. She told her husband of her decision to be content and he was relieved. She had not realized that her constant talk about babies had made him feel insecure and inadequate. They both agreed to stop concentrating on this one problem in life and focus on what was good in their marriage. As they accepted their situation as it was, they began to relax. She had not known how much emotional energy she was using in this intense concentration on reproduction. Three weeks after her decision to be content, she got pregnant. She was so excited to tell me the news and she added, "Keep telling women to accept their situations and learn to be content. God works much quicker in an accepting and relaxed human being."

> God grant me the serenity
> to accept the things I cannot change;
> courage to change the things I can;
> and wisdom to know the difference.
> Reinhold Niebuhr

Carol Kent, C.L.A.S.S. staff member from Michigan, gives her testimony on self-image. She recalls the day in grammar school when the little boys were laughing at her and she heard one say, "You're right, she does have big lips." She went home crying and tried to come up with ways to "pull in" her lips. She grew up fearful that friends would make fun of her lips, and some did. Here was something she couldn't do anything about and as she matured she learned to accept the looks God had given her. Instead of sitting tight-lipped in a corner, Carol has used her story as a message of hope for others.

How about you? Can you throw away the incorrect assessments you've had of yourself? Are you willing to change areas that really need improvement? God says you are acceptable unto Him just the way you are, so don't let the past ruin your future.

It Takes So Little To Be ABOVE AVERAGE.

4

Bring Out the Best

Anxiety in a man's heart weighs him down, but a good word makes him glad.

Proverbs 12:25 (RSV)

As I was speaking on depression in a Texas town, I asked how many could remember a specific childhood incident when someone had said something that really hurt, something that stamped a deep negative impression onto the mind. Almost every hand went up. I asked those willing to share to stand up, and many told of past experiences that were still real in their minds today.

One lady remembered how her father wanted a boy and how he had frequently said, "You'd have been all right if you'd been a boy." One girl told of the teacher who often asked her, "How did you ever get into the gifted program? You sure don't belong here." One woman in elegant and expensive clothes came up after the lecture and confessed, "I've been verbally abusing my two children and I didn't realize it until today."

When we look objectively at others and listen to their pain, we can see how thoughtless comments made to children have lasting, damaging results. Lately we have heard so much about anorexia nervosa, a "new" ailment where the victim literally starves to death. The sufferer is usually a young woman obsessed with having a slim body. Any obsession is abnormal, but this one leads to a critical body condition. Why do girls starve themselves? Why do they still diet when they have lost 40% of their body weight? Dr. Jean Mayer gives this answer:

> Obviously, anorexia nervosa does not begin with compulsive dieting. A psychological history often shows that the girl was chubby or downright fat, and that the drive to start dieting had been triggered by a disparaging remark about weight from someone whose opinion was highly valued, usually an older man.[1]

What damage a "disparaging remark" can cause! We must realize the power each one of us has in the tongue. We can use our words to build up or we can use them to tear down. A leader should encourage others. A leader must give hope.

In Proverbs 25:11 it says, "A word fitly spoken is like apples of gold in pictures of silver." We use this verse as our C.L.A.S.S. motto, aiming to be clear, constructive, and complimentary in every word we say. Ephesians 4:29 warns us to

> Let no corrupt communication proceed out of your mouth, but that which is good to the use of edifying, that it may minister grace unto the hearers.

How simple it sounds to say only those words which will edify and build up the listener. How we would like each one of our words to minister grace or do a favor for the hearer. One day I was attending a church service and was asked on the spot to give a children's sermon. I stood before rows of young people and taught them Ephesians 4:29 from memory. As I broke it into parts, I asked, "What does it mean to 'minister grace'?"

A boy accurately stated, "Do a favor."

"What else?" I asked and a little girl said, "It's like giving someone a present full of words."

I loved her simple concept and asked the children to think of their conversation as opportunities to give presents to their friends. "From here on, when you open your mouth, picture each word as a little gift, wrapped up in pretty paper with a crisp bow on top."

How about you? Are your words presents? When you speak to your child, your parent, your mate, do you do them a favor?

It takes no time, trouble, or thought to be critical. It just comes naturally, but oh how it can hurt! In a recent seminar Dr. William Glasser was heard to say that over 90% of all break-ups in human relationships are because of criticism. We hate to receive it, but we seem to enjoy dishing it out, breaking the spirit of those around us.

> *A merry heart doeth good like a medicine: but a broken spirit drieth the bones.*
>
> *Proverbs 17:22*

> *Pleasant words are as an honeycomb, sweet to the soul, and health to the bones.*
>
> *Proverbs 16:24*

Could you make a commitment today to cease criticizing others and drying up their bones? Could you make a prayerful effort to use pleasant words sweet to the soul? Could you become a traveling physician dispensing pieces of your merry heart, doing good like a medicine?

Bonnie Green was telling our C.L.A.S.S. about several visits she had made to the home of the Kennedys. I asked her, "What was there about that family that turned out so many leaders?"

She replied, "It was because the father and mother encouraged their children to greatness." She told of a certain night when she sat at the dinner table and Father Kennedy asked her a question beyond her ability to answer. She pulled the best thought she could from her resources and made a statement. As she finished Mr. Kennedy looked her straight in the eye and said, "That was a brilliant answer. May I quote you on this?" Bonnie never forgot that moment. "The Kennedys had the ability to *bring out the best* in others."

How I want to be that kind of person, not one who dries up the bones, but one who brings out the best in others. We don't stop to realize the harm we can do with our words. But as we have reviewed how others have hurt our self-image in the past, we want to be careful that we aren't doing the same thing. I have learned from available statistics that we tend to repeat the mistakes of our parents. For example, a boy who was beaten by his father, hated every minute of mistreatment and vowed he'd never lay a hand on his son, grows up to beat his child. Our intellect tells us not to do these negative things, but when we are in a stressful situation, we react emotionally as our parents did in the same set of circumstances. We don't map out our feelings, we just react instantly.

If we were told as children we were dummies, we tend to pass this on to our children. Isn't it time to break the chain?

Bill Glass, who is involved in prison ministry, asked a group of inmates how many had parents who had told them that they were stupid and would end up in jail? One hundred percent raised their hands in affirmation. What does this story teach us? That the words and attitudes we put into our children is what they will reproduce. We plant seeds today that will become the flowers or weeds of tomorrow. Currently we hear much about computers and we know that the machine can produce no information that has not been put into it—"Garbage in, garbage out." If you feed it negative material it will spew out negative answers.

Look at the mind of your child as a little computer. What material are you feeding into it? What caustic comments from you will create an inferiority complex in your child? We are programming these computers for their future reactions. Are you laying foundations for a creative mind or a critical tongue? What they *hear* now is what they'll *say* later.

> There is one whose rash words are like sword thrusts, but the tongue of the wise brings healing.
>
> Proverbs 12:18 (RSV)

When my daughter Marita was 18 and in a rebellious stage, I determined to pour my life into her in such a way that she would want to stay in the fold. I told her daily how much I loved her and what a joy she was to my life. I did not criticize her clothes or companions and made all her friends welcome in our home. I took her with me on speaking trips and, while she appeared disinterested in what I was teaching, the words were going into her computer. She liked the excitement of traveling and she accepted "listening to Mother" as paying her way.

Once I said to her,"I can envision the two of us as speaking together: you doing outer beauty and me doing inner beauty." Years later she reminded me of my statement and let me know what her reaction had been at the time. She had made no comment then but had said to herself, "That will be the day when I spend my time in churches with women!"

We continued to spend our time in churches with women. Marita listened to my speaking, my Bible teaching, and my counseling. At the end of each day I would go over the life stories of the different women and ask her what she thought each should do to overcome her problems. Whatever she came up with as an answer, I would compliment her on her sound thinking.

One day she announced, "I want to travel with you all the time. What should I do to get ready?" Marita had always had an eye for color. Her college courses were in design and she had become a sharp and stylish dresser. We found customized training for her and she became a color consultant. When I was asked to speak at women's retreats, I would volunteer Marita as a special feature on fashion and they would be glad to get a free bonus. As she spoke to women I would evaluate her performance. She had a teachable spirit and soon her ability moved from adequate to ABOVE AVERAGE.

Some time later Marita told me, "When I'm doing color consultations with ladies, they start telling me their marriage problems and I'm just amazed at the answers I give them. I've never been married and yet I open my mouth and out comes the right advice. Then I realized it's your words, Mother, that I'm saying. It's my mouth, but it's your advice. Those years of filling me up have paid off."

How grateful I am that Marita has stored up more information from her Christian mother than from atheistic professors. The Bible tells us that when we as "virtuous women" have done what we should do, our children will rise up and call us blessed (Proverbs 31:28). Marita has chosen to follow in my footsteps and that is blessing enough for me.

Never underestimate the power you have to program the computer mind in your child. What you put in will later come out. Do not give up because your child doesn't hang on your every word. They don't even want you to know they've heard what you've said, but *they have*. Keep feeding the machine.

> *Train up a child in the way he should go: and when he is old, he will not depart from it.*
>
> Proverbs 22:6

How much of what goes into your child's mind comes from you? How much comes from the mother down the street? From a babysitter? From friends? From teachers? From television?

The Bible tells us we are responsible for training our children diligently when we walk or sit and even when we lie down and rise up (Deuteronomy 6:7). That's *all the time!* What are you doing with your children? Are you critical or complimentary? Do you lift up or knock down? Do you bring out the best or the worst?

In a eulogy to the late Paul "Bear" Bryant, famous Alabama football coach, *Newsweek* (February 7, 1983) said he:

> ...Always held some secret or strategy or winning edge that nobody quite figured out.... It's hard to guess whether the Bear would rather be remembered for the god-like image or the human virtues. Come to think of it, he would probably approach the problem the way he did the rest of football and life. He'd settle for the best of everything.

Truly, Bear Bryant with 323 wins was "the best" and he brought out the best of everything in others. Why don't you practice bringing out the best in others? If you want your child to be ABOVE AVERAGE, check the quality of the material you're putting into the brain. He can't give out with anything better than the accumulation of what has gone in. Feed him frequently, nourish him well; for what goes in today is what will come out tomorrow.

It Takes So Little To Be ABOVE AVERAGE.

5

Accept the Best

Not one of us wants to be criticized, yet we seem equally uncomfortable with praise. Some of us have been knocked down so long that we don't feel we deserve a compliment and some of us doubt that any positive person is really telling the truth. Where does this negative attitude place the positive person? How does this kind and uplifting individual feel when he has given a compliment and the recipient's response ranges from uneasy silence to vehement denial?

How would I feel if I saw you in a royal purple gown at the president's reception and said, "What a beautiful gown. You look like a queen in purple!" and you returned, "Look like a queen? Are you crazy? I look more like the maid."? You have now let me know I'm stupid and wouldn't know a queen if I were standing in Buckingham Palace.

How about a hypothetical compliment: "That's a lovely linen suit you're wearing today." Some possible responses:

—"This old thing?"
—"This isn't linen; it's just rayon."
—"I picked it up at Goodwill."
—"It's a reject from my sister."

Any of these comments show I have no taste and remind me never to say a nice word to you again.

Many ladies complain that their husbands never give them

compliments. One man summed it up when he said, "I used to tell her how good she looked and she'd always make me feel like a dummy for saying so. Finally I quit noticing anything and now she complains."

A dentist complimented his receptionist, "Your hair looks great today."

She retorted, "What was wrong with it yesterday?"

We mean to be humble but we insult the intelligence of the givers when we refuse their compliments. How much happier we can make others when we express gratitude for their comments. A simple thank you is sufficient but if you wish to make a positive addition, that is even better.

"Your hair always looks attractive."
"Thank you. I'm really pleased with my hairdresser at Plaza Place."

• • •

"I love your black dress."
"Thank you. My husband picked it out especially for this occasion."

• • •

"Your new outfit is the latest style."
"Thank you. Coming from someone with your taste, I especially appreciate your comment."

• • •

"You play piano beautifully."
"Thank you. My years of practice have finally paid off."

Accept each compliment as you would a present, words wrapped up in a box with a bow on top. Say thank you and you'll receive more; reject the praise and you'll soon receive none.

It Takes So Little To Be ABOVE AVERAGE.

6

Accept the Worst

Now that we are all able to accept compliments, what should we do about accepting criticism? Not one of us loves to hear what's wrong with us; no normal person looks to be hurt. We all wish our friends and family loved us unconditionally, as they should, but we are all realistic enough to know that many people feel led to give us some "constructive criticism." Proverbs 12:16 (TLB) says, "A fool is quick-tempered; but a wise man stays cool when insulted." Ignoring an insult is easier said than done. How can we learn to handle harsh words?

Since I always teach from my own experiences, let me share how I developed a plan for accepting the worst. As I analyzed my dislike for negative evaluations, I determined I would *learn to "take it."* I would grit my teeth and accept whatever was dumped on me. This "keep your mouth shut" attitude kept me out of trouble, but it didn't calm my turbulent insides. The more active I became in the speaking world, the more criticism I received. I became a believer of James' statement, "Let not many of you become teachers...for you know that we who teach shall be judged with greater strictness" (James 3:1 RSV). I decided "taking it" wasn't enough; I had to take it cheerfully. As I prayed about the ability to do this, the Lord showed me I had to *be thankful for each comment.* You mean, say thank you for criticism?

Let's think about this possibility. What does the person who gives you unsolicited advice expect from you? He expects you will become defensive, lose your Christian cool, and therefore validate his opinion that you have a problem and aren't practicing what you preach. Since you don't want to give him this affirmation of his evaluation, accept his advice cheerfully and thank him for it. This stops him in his tracks in a most positive way and prevents him from proceeding to Points B, C, and D.

In pursuing this plan, I have developed some helpful answers without resorting to lying. I may not think much of the idea but I can always say: "Thank you for sharing that thought with me"; "Thank you for the time you put into this analysis"; "Thank you for caring enough to point that out"; "I appreciate your thoughts and I will surely discuss them with the staff"; "I must say I have never considered that before, but I will give your suggestion some thought."

All of these comments are positive and true and will deal with the critic cheerfully. As you become good at accepting criticism and develop your own style of response, you can then move on to the third step: *Ask for it.* That step is the graduate work in our Christian living. We feel we've made progress when we can first take it, then take it cheerfully. But when the Lord is really in control of our lives, He will prompt us to ask for it. So often in Proverbs it says that a wise man asks for counsel while a fool despises instruction and that if you rebuke a wise man he will love you, but a fool will hate you. If a wise man loves rebuke and I want to be wise, I must look for helpful suggestions. I must ask for evaluation.

As I perceived this plan as a path to wisdom, my defensive attitude disappeared and I developed a spiritual willingness to seek counsel. I don't want to be one of Solomon's fools. Indeed, "Better is a poor and a wise child than an old and foolish king, who will no more be admonished" (Ecclesiastes 4:13).

So ask yourself three questions:

1. Are you willing to take criticism?
2. Are you willing to take it cheerfully?
3. Are you willing to ask for it?

Let's assume you wish to be wise and not foolish. What should you do when you receive a critical comment, admonishing advice, or a scathing scenario? First, you swallow hard and take it. Then you smile, if possible, and instead of defending yourself, thank the person for caring enough to share these thoughts with you. Let him know you will take these ideas to heart and give them consideration. If you're ready for graduate work, ask for some further help or suggestions.

Now that you've passed your finals, what do you do with this new information? You run it through the "fact filter" in your mind and determine: If it's wise, true, and applicable, act upon it. If it's foolish, false, and ridiculous, forget it. How do you know the difference? Ask the Lord to guide you. If when you test, "Am I sarcastic?" some clear examples come to your mind, you should accept this possibility and work prayerfully to overcome your tendency to make humor at others' expense. If someone says, "You'd look a lot better if you'd smile once in a while," ask a close friend if you need to smile more. If she hesitates in answering, you'll know this is a problem you need to work on.

What if you sift it through the "fact filter" and it makes no sense at all? You say, "Lord, if this thought is as foolish as it appears to be, help me to forget it."

> . . . *A wise man's heart discerneth both time and judgement.*
> *Ecclesiastes 8:5*

After speaking at a retreat of 3000 women in Michigan, I received a large envelope with the audience evaluations of my performance. I read each one and found the majority to be extremely positive. Several mentioned that the second half of a skit I had produced was too long. I listened to that tape with this thought in mind, and agreed it was too long. I profited from these comments and improved the product.

One lady wrote, "Florence was unexpectedly exciting, which goes to show appearances are deceiving." When I ran this through my mind, I came up confused. I was glad I was exciting, but I wasn't sure what had been deceptive about my appearance. I'll never know, but I surely shouldn't waste much time brooding over this evaluation.

Let's learn to accept suggestions and even insults cheerfully. Let's ask for evaluations and listen thankfully. Let's run them through our mental "fact filter." If they're valid, let's act upon them. If they're of no consequence, let's forget them.

Former Chief Justice Charles Evans Hughes once said, "If you can accept and profit by criticism, you have a priceless ability possessed by few of your fellow men."

Patsy Clairmont is an exceptional communicator and gifted humorist. She has, however, been very weak and in poor health. Many of the staff were concerned about her and it fell upon me to make some suggestions. Her initial reaction was defensive as is natural, but the next evening when I went to my hotel room there was a note on my pillow. "Thank you for caring enough about my health to make suggestions." Through these suggestions she was put on a positive program which has led her up the long road to improved physical strength and stamina.

When we can accept and profit from what we didn't want to hear, we do have a priceless ability possessed by few.

It Takes So Little To Be ABOVE AVERAGE.

7

Win the Blue Ribbon

I've always wanted to be a winner! Many years ago as I was raising my children, I also raised roses. I entered cuttings in the Women's Club Flower Show and won. What does it take for a rose to be a winner? She doesn't just sit there on her slim stem in the sun and excel. She needs care and sometimes it hurts.

One day I went to a pruning demonstration at Flowerland and learned some basic principles which I remember clearly today.

1. The purpose of pruning is to improve the quality of the roses, not to hurt the bush.
2. Pruning should not be started until the gardener has a clear picture in mind of what he wants the finished product to look like. Since the aim is to make the branches form the shape of an urn, everything should be removed that does not conform to the ultimate plan.
3. Cut off all branches and twigs that stick out sideways and do not enhance the urn-like shape.
4. Prune out branches in the center that are rubbing against each other, that are at cross purposes, that are choking out the air.
5. Clip closely any sucker shoots that are growing wildly and sapping the energy from the plant.
6. Make sure your shears are sharp so you won't tear up the branches as you cut them.

As I was preparing a C.L.A.S.S. lesson on being able to take criticism, this whole pruning demonstration came quickly to my mind. In John 15 we are told that Jesus is the vine, we are the branches and God is the gardener. He prunes off every branch that doesn't bear fruit and he prunes each one that does so that it will bear more. Suddenly I saw a comparison.

Picture yourself as a rosebush. You have produced flowers in the past, but God the Gardener knows you could blossom even more. To make you bloom to your full potential, to make you a blue-ribbon winner, He must prune off all that's keeping you from the prize. Let's review the pruning principles and see how they relate to us.

1. Pruning is not punishment but purposeful planning. God is not cutting you to hurt you, but to produce perfection.

2. God the Gardener already has in mind what he wants you to look like. He has a plan for your ultimate use and only He has the picture of the finished product. When you get rebuffed in one area, stopped in one pursuit, cut by a friend, God knows it hurts but He knows it is necessary to bring you into his purposeful planning, to shape you like that open vessel.

3. When God, who holds the blueprint, gazes down upon us, He sees branches that are sticking out with no rhyme or reason, pursuits in our life that are without eternal values, selfish goals that detract from our spiritual shape. He needs to cut these off, but since He doesn't stroll around our garden with big pruning shears, He sends people to do it for Him, friends who tell us things "for our own good," mates who point out how much time we're wasting, mothers-in-law who show us how they did it better. Some bushes don't take this pruning kindly and they never bear much fruit. Some accept the cuts, learn from the comments, and go on to win the prize.

4. Since God's purpose is to produce an open vessel ready to be filled with His Holy Spirit, He needs to empty out all that's cluttering up our lives. He sees branches that are rubbing against each other causing friction in our relationships and He has to clip them out. He sees activities that are at cross purposes keeping us busy in all directions but achieving little. He sees projects that are positive but are pulling us away from His plan. He sees anger, bitterness, jealousy and other negative emotions which are choking out our spiritual air so

we are gasping for breath. He sends His saints with His scissors to shape us up and sometimes we refuse to be shorn.

5. Have you ever watched a sucker shoot grow? Recently I had one that touched the roof. One week it wasn't there and the next week it was ten feet high. It shot off in a flash, using up every ounce of strength the poor bush had. Healthy leaves shriveled up and buds drooped their little heads. Often we beautiful rosebushes allow sucker shoots to run rampant. We have projects, problems, or pressures that take over our lives, grow out of control and drain our energy dry. Unpruned, these shoots so sap our strength that we have no stamina left. God the Gardener knows a sucker shoot when He sees one and He sends His angels to warn us that we're springing off in the wrong direction, that we need to call a quick halt to this unproductive growth.

6. As God trains His little helpers who come to clip us, He asks them to use sharp shears so we won't be torn up in the process of pruning. However, as with every profession in life, some are slow learners and inflict more pain than others. But once we accept God's program—***Pruning is not punishment but purposeful planning***—we can absorb the cutting cheerfully and ultimately ask for it.

Do you want your roses to win the prize? Take a moment to evaluate your own life and ask yourself if each principle has become your way of thinking.

1. Know that pruning is for a purpose and that the sooner you accept it, the less it will hurt.

2. Know that God has a visual plan for your life. He can picture what you'll look like when He's brought you into full bloom. He's pruning you to conform you to His image.

3. Know that if God wants to use you in a special way, He will send gardeners to cut off those wasted projects, to tone down your harsh words, to improve your looks. Don't fight off the critics; listen and learn.

4. Know that God sees what's inside you. He grieves that you're bickering with your children and carrying on conflict for control with your spouse. He wants to sort out your cluttered mind and blow away the chaff. He pleads with you to empty

out your bitterness and strife and let Him fill you with His Spirit: love, joy, peace, patience, kindness, goodness, faithfulness, humility, and self-control (Galatians 5:22).

5. Know that each one of us has a sucker shoot at one time or another and ask yourself what it is that's draining strength from your life. If you can cut it off yourself before the gardener gets there, it won't hurt so much. Do you spend too much time at church and too little at home? Are you exhausted by five o'clock each day and disagreeable at dinner? Are your projects and philanthropies more show than substance? What's your sucker shoot? Self-pruning is painless if you do it quickly.

6. Know that not all pruners have been sent by God; some people go into this business on their own. Listen to their words, run them through your "fact finder," and let God say, "Right on" or "Ridiculous."

When God sends His workers they will be there not for punishment but for purposeful planning. So the next time you look up and see that lady approaching who loves to cut you down, smile cheerfully, ask for her advice, and pray that her shears are sharp.

It Takes So Little To Be ABOVE AVERAGE.

B

It Takes So Little To Think Above Average

8

Realize We Don't Think Much

It doesn't take much to think ABOVE AVERAGE because the average person doesn't think much. Henry James, the turn-of-the-century psychologist, said that the average person uses only 10% of his available brain power. Do you see how little extra you would have to think to be ABOVE AVERAGE? If you exerted only 2% beyond your norm, you'd be on your way; if you doubled your thinking capacity, you'd be close to brilliant!

It sounds so simple. Why aren't we all thinking our way to success?

The first reason is that we didn't know we *weren't* doing it. We thought we were thinking. When I first started teaching my C.L.A.S.S. I had no lesson on thinking. I assumed we all knew how to do that. Since we were a group of Christian leaders, certainly we must be thinkers. As the seminar grew, I began to get an amazing and consistent reaction: "I didn't know I could think this hard"; "I didn't realize my brain wasn't really working"; "My mind hasn't been turned on for fourteen years."

As I became aware that individuals were learning to think in our seminar (and I wasn't even teaching the subject), I wondered what would happen if I began to teach it—and how I would approach it.

The average person has always been a little afraid of deep thinkers, mystics or ivory tower people. As Julius Caesar said, "Yond Cassius has a lean and hungry look; He thinks too much: such men are dangerous."[1]

We don't want to be peculiar; we want to be relevant. Surely, we are not like Cassius in thinking too much. When my son was in sixth grade I found as I questioned him about his English homework that he didn't know a noun from a verb. Having been an English teacher, I was aghast that he had somehow missed "parts of speech." I went to his teacher at the Christian school he attended and asked her where Fred had been when she taught nouns. Her answer was, "We don't teach those things anymore. No one really needs to know them to get along in life." She was right in one way. Fred doesn't know them and he is still alive.

If you don't know a noun and verb, you can't know a clause. If you don't know a clause, you don't know how to punctuate. If you can't place a comma or a period in the right spot, your sentences all run together. No wonder most high school graduates can't construct a complete paragraph and need their mothers to write their college application letters.

Seven years after I realized that the simple basics of education were not being taught to my son, the National Commission on Excellence in Education came out with a scathing report on the present condition of our schools. "A tide of mediocrity has devastated public education. If an unfriendly foreign power had attempted to impose on America the mediocre educational performance that exists today, we might well have viewed it as an act of war."[2]

Carolyn Kane, in an inspired article, "Thinking: A Neglected Art," writes:

> Intelligence is just as much a part of human nature as sociability. It would certainly be unnatural for a person to allow his mind to die of neglect....
>
> ...If we are to survive as a free people, we will have to take some courses of action as soon as possible, because regardless of what some advertisers have led us to believe, this country does not run on oil. It runs on ideas.[3]

I remember my freshman year in high school when I had to take Latin. No one wanted to take Latin; we had to if we wanted to go to college. We complained and murmured, "Why do we have to take Latin? It's a dead language."

One morning, no one seemed to have completed the Latin assignment. The teacher, Miss McCormick, wasted no words. "How many of you decided this lesson was too hard for you?" We raised our hands. "Were there any of you who did it?" To our amazement several hands went up. Miss McCormick called these spoilers up and read their scripts back and forth with them. Simple, sensible sentences. We could all understand them.

When the exercise was over she kept these students up front and stated, "In every group there are always a limited few who are ABOVE AVERAGE. The majority of you did the average thing. You decided the assignment was unfair and too difficult. You had no trouble finding friends whose goals were no higher than your own. These students before you also knew the lesson was close to impossible, but they decided to do it anyway. They pushed their minds beyond their past abilities and they achieved results. Are you going to spend your lives being average and supporting yourselves with excuses or are you going to be among those few who achieve the impossible?"

We were all humbled, disliking those few who had been praised, but we stopped looking for legitimate ways out of our Latin lessons and within the month we were all conversing in simple Latin sentences.

Have I ever needed to speak Latin? No. Was that year wasted time because it wasn't practical? Oh, no. I learned Latin roots, prefixes, and suffixes that doubled my English vocabulary and which have served me well ever since, but most of all I learned to stretch my mind beyond the possible to ABOVE AVERAGE.

Today very few students have to take Latin or learn to diagram a sentence. We are keeping much of our education practical. As the Commission on Excellence stated in their report, our schools are offering "a cafeteria-style curriculum in which the appetizers and desserts can easily be mistaken for the main course."[4]

When Marita was a senior in high school, she took two units of work experience which meant she got credit for waitressing in a coffee shop while gathering in tips. She also participated in "Community Lab" where it was suggested she visit city hall and the county museum at any convenient time. This was surely a cafeteria-style curriculum.

Recently the State of California came up with a unique thought: Why not make up a competency test for new teachers? To check its validity they gave the test to current teachers and the newspaper headlines reflected the public's shock when they proclaimed that many of the present teachers couldn't pass the competency test in their own subject. When the standards are low enough, it takes almost nothing to be ABOVE AVERAGE.

If we wish to raise the level of our thinking power, we first have to recognize that we don't really think much. We tend to *do* a lot and *think* a little. We feel that intellectual activity is akin to laziness; we don't see tangible results from meditation.

My mother, having struggled for survival through the Depression, doesn't understand work that isn't "normal." My brother Ron is the top radio personality in Dallas and he spends much of his time thinking up ways to keep his station "Number One." His office is a dimly-lit room where he can lean back in a comfortable chair and "let the muses float free." After visiting him my mother said, "I can't believe he even earns money sitting around thinking up those tom-fool ideas! I wonder if he'll ever grow up and get a real job."

Thinking doesn't show and its results later appear to be momentary flashes. Thinking takes time and determination.

Carol Kane says:

> Even Einstein had to study and think for months before he could formulate his theory of relativity. Those of us who are less intelligent find it a struggle to conceive even a moderately good idea, let alone a brilliant one.[5]

Are we basically agreed that we don't think a lot? Then what should we do about it?

It Takes So Little To Be ABOVE AVERAGE.

9

Decide to Improve Our Minds

The Bible tell us, "As [a man] thinketh in his heart, so is he" (Proverbs 23:7). This verse explains why those of us who don't think much don't amount to much and demonstrates the power the mind has over the body. Abraham Lincoln said, "A man's about as happy as he sets out to be." The human mind is amazingly open to suggestions and it will grasp onto whatever we feed it.

When we tell our minds we will fail, we often do. As our schools have dropped the basics from their curricula in order to teach practical skills and brotherly love, they have instead ironically produced bodies that can't think and people who don't even like each other. Brotherly love and busing in place of basics simply hasn't worked. The school report shows:

> Each generation of Americans has outstripped its parents in education, in literacy and in economic attainment. For the first time in the history of our country, the educational skills of one generation will not surpass, will not equal, will not even approach, those of their parents.[1]

Response to this shocking evaluation has stirred a flood of protest and the *Los Angeles Times* has been printing letters on "The Sorry State of U.S. Schooling." Karen Chrisney of Arcadia, wrote, "I believe that more mind-stimulating lessons should take the place of the tedious 'busy work,' which is all writing and very little thinking. In fact, a greater number of students might actually do their homework if it were more appealing to them."[2]

As we have drifted away from the basics of thought-provoking education and have dropped discipline for free-thinking, no one is thinking at all. Don Bresnahan, producer of TV documentaries for KABC, Los Angeles, wrote in *Newsweek*, "People don't want to think seriously or for very long." He tells how he formerly produced "serious issue-oriented half-hour and hour-long documentaries." But the Nielson ratings showed that the public didn't want anything so deep. "They tell us that you viewers have an attention span of no more than a minute to a minute and a half. That's why we race from story to story, giving you peaks and valleys.... If we don't tell our stories quickly and necessarily briefly, we might lose you to some more frivolous activity like reading a book or brushing your teeth."[3] Now Mr. Bresnahan produces "minidocs": quick, easily-digested chunks spread out over five nights.

But the tide appears to be turning. I was amazed to find a drawing of a brain on the cover of *U.S. News and World Report* (January 24, 1983). Since cover subjects indicate interest of the general public, I was encouraged with their article dividing the brain into sections which control our emotions and telling us of new information on the power of the brain. Two weeks later (February 7, 1983), *Newsweek* had a cartoon head on their cover labeled, "The Human Computer—How the Brain Works." In April, *Reader's Digest* showed silhouetted heads full of numbers with their lead article, "Seven Steps to Better Thinking." *Forbes* (December 20, 1982) produced several pages on "How to Think Sideways," and that same month *The Toastmaster* applauded "Whole Mind Power."

Suddenly there seems to be an interest in the brain. *Newsweek* says:

> The mind has always been dumbfounded by the brain. That three-pound glob of matter hardly seems up to the task of writing "Paradise Lost," composing "Eroica" or discovering relativity. Yet for 2,400 years, ever since Hippocrates located the seat of the intellect inside the skull, the mind has been forced to admit that its greatest achievements, its loftiest thoughts, its

deepest emotions all arise from something with the consistency of Jell-O and the color of day-old slush.[4]

After pages of diagrams and detailed explanations they conclude:

Neuroscientists may have pulled memory and emotion
under their reductionist umbrella, argue the skeptics,
but surely will and consciousness will escape them. In
fact, the brain's very complexity will postpone the day
when it is finally explained by common forces.[5]

They've figured out many complexities of the brain but they
can't master the human will. God gave us our own free will and
no outside force can quickly change or even understand it.
Remember the story of the little boy whose mother made him sit
in the corner. He looked up and said, "I may be sitting on the
outside but I'm standing up inside."

Our will is within our own control. Are you going to determine
today to push it that extra mile toward discovery and creativity?
Let's assume you are a mature person who has recognized you
don't do a lot of deep thinking and who has decided to improve
your mind. What can you do about it? Ted Turner, chairman of
Turner Broadcasting System and owner of the Atlanta Braves and
Hawks, said in an interview, "I believe the brain is a muscle, and
like any other muscle, the more you use it the stronger it gets.
You almost have to teach yourself to think more."[6]

Whether you think of your brain as Jell-O, day-old slush, or a
muscle, you can agree that it's an amazing apparatus and it has
limitless possibilities. You don't have to understand it to appreciate
it.

One day in the middle of a speaking engagement I made the
statement that God does not waste any of our experiences in life.
At that same instant it came to me, "What about those years you
spent in playing bridge? What good have they done you as a Christian speaker?" While I was still speaking some remote parts of
my mind were having this discussion and I suddenly realized I
was able to talk and think on different tracks at the same time.
Instantly I answered my original question: Years of playing bridge
had taught me to think on four tracks—clubs, diamonds, hearts,
and spades! God had not wasted my ability to quickly file those
fifty-two cards in columns in my brain. The ability was still

intact; he had just changed the labels on the tracks.

On the way home that day, I asked myself what my present tracks were labeled? I now realized I was thinking of more than one thing at a time and this was surely an asset to my speaking, but what were my tracks doing? I had already been conducting C.L.A.S.S and I was constantly breaking the skills I had into teachable units so that I could communicate them to others. As I analyzed my thinking, I could see my first speaking track was full of material—subject matter from my life experiences, memories of my childhood, collections of prose and poetry I had studied, Bible verses I had learned.

My second track was my ability to outline my material ahead of time, to organize my thoughts, to shorten or change my order while speaking. As I thought of these two tracks I realized they were essential for effective elocution. Without something to say there would be no reason to speak. Without any organization there would be no way to remember the message.

Added to these two came my response track, the one that is open to the leadings of the Holy Spirit, hearing His voice of suggestions, and also responsible to the needs and attitudes of people. Without a firm hold on one's material and a simple outline to hold it all together, there'd be no opening for a responsible track.

When all three of these are working concurrently, there is a desire to communicate the inner feelings of one's conscience, one's emotions, one's heart to the listener. This genuine sharing of one's own life is what makes the hearers remember you as a person they can relate to and learn from.

As these simple concepts of how my brain worked appeared to me, I realized where the term "one-track mind" came from— people who could only hold one set of ideas together at a time. Have you met people with one-track minds? What a waste when we have limitless tracks available and waiting to be used.

As I began to teach those in the seminars to think on four tracks, we developed an acrostic to help us remember how to communicate more effectively:

M aterial

O rganization

R esponse

E motion

As Christians we need to be able to think MORE than we've been used to doing. You may not have checked your mind recently to find out what its potentials are but start stretching and training a four-track mind. *Time* recently said of defeated English labor leader, Michael Foot, "He displayed an impressive ability to talk for hours without a text, but his train of thought was occasionally derailed."[7]

It Does Take Something to be ABOVE AVERAGE.

10

Set Aside a Think Spot

Before we can get down to actually improving our minds, we should set aside some spot where we can think quietly and uninterrupted. Because we don't take the time and effort to remove ourselves from the confusion of life, we have difficulty doing much creative thinking. The Lord Jesus taught us the value of withdrawing to a quiet place to pray and to think. Do you have such a spot? Do you already have a place for your daily quiet time? If not, this might be the start of something new.

Some have a desk, a corner table, an easy chair. One girl I know drives to a camellia garden, one walks by the shore, one sits in her car overlooking the city. My favorite spot is in my bathroom. I have a tub with a carpeted step up to it and I lay my Bible there and sit on the floor. A ledge behind the tub holds pots of African violets and the window opens into a plant-filled atrium. This spot is beautiful to look at and peaceful to my soul. It is here that I've prayed through some difficult times in my life. It is a special place where I can be still and know that He is Almighty God.

Airplanes are "think spots" for me also. When I finish a three-day C.L.A.S.S. and sink into a seat on the plane, I am alone, able to sort out the seminar, able to jot down creative ideas and improvements before I forget them.

Robert Anderson, chairman of Atlantic-Richfield says:

Flying has provided a major part of the time that I can

> devote to thinking. It is an isolated environment; there
> are no telephones, and there is no way anyone can in-
> trude on your thoughts.[1]

Anne Ortland, in her book *Disciplines of a Beautiful Woman*, em-
phasizes the need for a daily quiet time and she frequently goes
to a restaurant to spend some reflective moments. Once a month
she and her husband Ray go away for a special day of thinking.

Many of you may want to combine your daily devotions with
your thinking time. God asks that we put Him first, give Him our
first 10%. As we pray and read God's Word, we can open our
minds to His direction and let His thoughts stimulate ours. "Let
this mind be in you which was also in Christ Jesus."[2]

As we begin to realize how little time we spend in solitary
meditation, is it any wonder our brain is only functioning at one-
tenth of its potential? If you wish to speed up your thinking process, start by finding a "think spot" and setting aside time to use
it. Once you find how much fun it is to expand your creative
ability, you will see "think spots" everywhere: in your car, in line
at the supermarket, in the dentist's waiting room, in church. Make
use of them, think constantly.

It Takes So Little To Be ABOVE AVERAGE.

11

Start With the Past

Picture your brain as a file cabinet. Since statistics show we are using only one-tenth of our available mental space, let's be specific. Let's picture our brain as a large file cabinet with ten drawers. The bottom one is jammed with assorted information in no particular order. The facts aren't even in manila folders. Some thoughts are so old the edges have turned yellow and some new ideas are sitting outside the drawer in a pile waiting to be sorted out. Above this one eclectic drawer are nine empty ones. Once in awhile after a brilliant lecture you put a piece of the program in an empty drawer intending to go back and add to the subject later, but you've been so busy with the basics of life that you only have one drawer in operation, that bottom one labeled "Average."

There's so much brain space available yet we've crowded everything we know into one drawer. Where do we begin? We dedicate our thinking time to an introspective view of the past. Let's put our former life experiences into folders and label them for quick access when needed. We're told our brain contains everything we've ever seen or heard, but some of our memory is so remote we can't put our hands on the facts. If we wish to stir up our reservoir of knowledge, that wealth of information we have stored away, we must reminisce, pull the color out of the confusion and start using some of the empty drawers.

In C.L.A.S.S. we have a lesson on "How You Filled Your

Reservoir in the Past," where we list some items that will jog your memory. As you are reading these ideas, jot down the incidents that come to your mind. If you were to read this list over every day, you would still come up with new thoughts. Each time I teach this lesson, I remember new colorful examples from the past to add to *my* reservoir.

At first you may see no use in rehashing old events, but as you begin to reach for the past, your brain will throw itself in high gear and begin working in a new way. You'll be amazed at what you remember when you try. If you do any kind of speaking, such as teaching a Bible study, you will be excited over the fascinating examples you can find from your own life. If you do any writing, this mental exercise will stir your creative juices. Why not take a notebook and title each page with one of these headings? As you begin to fill in the blank pages, you will increase your reservoir, and will actually compile a biographical sketch of your life. These twelve pages from the *past* will inspire you to journalize the *present* as we will discuss in the *future*.

As I list the topics, let your mind wander. Pause for a few moments, write down what appears. Don't rush, relax.

Hometown Atmosphere: Where did you grow up? What kind of a town was it? What was your house like? How did it differ from the homes of your friends? Were there any special places to play or hide? What positive memory do you have of your environment?

I lived in three rooms behind my father's store in Haverhill, Massachusetts, a shoe factory town, recently chosen by a Rand-McNally survey as the least-desirable city in which to live in the entire United States. As children we ate our meals in front of the customers, and to go from one bedroom where all five of us slept in layers to the bathroom, we had to pass the cash register. All my friends had regular houses and in my teen years I was embarrassed to live in a store. Behind us were two garages and when my brothers went out to play with cars they *really* played with cars. In spite of the disadvantages, we all learned how to get along with people since we lived with them from six-thirty in the morning until eleven o'clock at night, seven days a week.

Nationality Blends: What kind of yarns are you woven from? Are you all one stock or are you a mixed breed? Does your background have any influence over your personality or current lifestyle? What nationality blends do your children have?

My father was born in England. He taught me poems, stories, and tongue twisters from the time I was very young and constantly stretched my imagination. His emphasis on language and vocabulary has had a definite impact on my life and that of my two brothers. My mother is Scotch-Canadian and as a child wore kilts and marched in a bagpipe band beside her father. Since my husband is German, my children are one-quarter English, one-quarter Scotch, and one-half German.

Childhood Relationships: What do you remember about your feelings about your brothers and sisters? Was there a special friend who influenced your life?

I always wanted a sister and little Jim was so beautiful that I would dress him up in my old clothes and pretend he was a girl. When my brother Ron was born I was so upset that *he* was a boy that I took him to the top of our street in his carriage, and then let it wheel freely into the traffic. Gratefully, the carriage hit a tree and was safely stopped. The incident so frightened me that I became slavishly devoted to my baby brother.

My girlfriend Peggy was everything I wanted to be. She had a turned-up nose and long thick blonde hair. She was popular at school and lived in a real house. When we went window shopping I would wait until she said what was pretty and then agree with her.

Are you beginning to have an idea of how to review and record your past? Do you see how easy it is to stimulate your brain into resourceful thinking? Now you fill in the remaining topics without my giving you examples.

Education and Other Training: How far back can you remember in your schooling? Who's the first teacher you can recall? Can you remember anything she taught you? What kind of a grammar school did you go to? What was your high school like? Was there any special teacher who influenced your life? Did you take any outside training? Did you win any contests, letters, or awards?

Talents and Hobbies: What kind of talent did you have as a child? Did you take any lessons? How did your parents compare your talent with theirs? With your brothers and sisters? Did your early talent have any bearing on your career? What hobbies have you had in life? How have they been productive in the past? Is there any talent you really wish you'd had?

Odd Jobs and Careers: What was your first job? What kind of a boss did you have? What did you learn from it? What was your most unusual job? Which job helped you shape your career choice? What career changes have you had in your adult career?

Courtship and Marriage: Where did you and your mate meet and under what circumstances? What differences did you have in background, religion, personality? How did you first know your relationship was serious? Who proposed and where were you at the time? How long was your engagement and what can you remember of this romantic time in your life? Where was the wedding held? What was the church or building like? What colors were the dresses? What flowers were carried? Where did you go on your honeymoon? What lessons did you learn in early marriage? What problems have you worked to overcome? What has been the most important bond between you and your partner?

Organizations and Leadership: List in sequence all the different groups you've been a part of up until now. Is there any consistency? Add next to each title any office you held in the group. Is there any similarity? Which organization did you most enjoy and why? Which did you contribute the most to and was this work appreciated? What leadership skills do you feel you have?

Churches Attended: List the different churches or denominations you have attended. What pastor can you remember best? What Sunday school teacher influenced your life and how? What church activities were you involved in such as choir, Sunday school teaching, missionary society? In retrospect, what quality of religious training did you receive? What lasting values have you retained from your church attendance?

Christian Commitment: When did you first commit your life to Jesus Christ? What made you realize you needed a savior? What person was influential in your decision? What changes has your commitment made on your life? How have you been sharing your faith with others? What Bible studies have you attended? Have you taught?

Family Circumstances: How old were you when your first child was born? Where were you living at the time? What circumstances changed in your marriage with the addition of children? What is special about each one of your children? Write a few sentences on each one. How has your life influenced their spiritual growth? Behavior? Education? Career choice?

Traumas, Illnesses and Victories: What is the most traumatic event of your life? In retrospect, what caused the situation? What was the most difficult part of the problem? What did you learn from it? List the major illnesses you've had. Which ones have had lasting effects on you? Have you had any difficult hospital experiences? What is your overall attitude on illness and poor health? In looking back over your life circumstances what have been your greatest victories? How could you share these experiences to give hope to others?

Once you have thoughtfully answered these questions in sequence, you will have enough recycled material to fill a whole drawer in your mental file cabinet. You will have these past thoughts brought up-to-date and they will be in order. You could turn this time of questioning yourself into a family activity. You could use one of these topics each night at dinner or each Sunday afternoon. You could include guests as everyone loves to tell stories of their youth, and you will learn things about your family and friends that you didn't know before.

Recently my son-in-law, Randy, sat down with my 85-year-old mother and asked her to reminisce about the old days. He had previously set up the video camera without her knowledge and she freely recalled her youth, marriage, attitudes about children, and personal feelings. What a blessing it will be to all of us to have her own words recorded for future generations.

We have received such excellent responses from C.L.A.S.S. members who have written us later to let us know what a meaningful experience it has been to record the events and feelings of the past. One lady typed hers all up, made copies, put them into folders, and gave one to each child for Christmas.

Take time to review your life and write it down. As you find a "think spot" and let your mind wander, ideas and life stories will come which you can add to your reservoir. Save these pages to insert into your journal (Chapter 13).

If you want to increase your mental ability, start with the past.

Don't be too busy with the present to reflect on the lessons of the past.

You are the world's greatest expert on you!

It Takes So Little To Be ABOVE AVERAGE.

12

Be Alert to the Present

So many people go through life with blinders on and heads down seeing none of the beauty or the events around them. With so little effort we can be alert and find excitement everywhere. I glean fascinating examples for my speaking every day in many ways. You, too, can become a much better conversationalist when you are alert to life.

One of my best sources of colorful material is the beauty shop. When I arrive the girls ask where I've been and where I'm going and soon all the customers are listening. To get new information I have only to throw out a topic and see what the reaction is. Everyone has something to say yet so few people have anyone who will listen.

One December I told them I was leaving for Oklahoma City to do a TV show on Christmas depression. Immediately a college girl told me so many students were depressed that the school had hired a psychologist to lecture on the subject. One lady volunteered that she became depressed each year when there was always a fight over which family to spend the day with, eventually everyone ending up mad during Christmas dinner. An elderly lady had tears in her eyes as she lamented she couldn't cook a big dinner any more and she had to depend on others. One girl had just moved to our area and was depressed because she couldn't afford to go home for Christmas. A widow confessed how she dreaded all holidays, and a young girl related how her brother had committed suicide on Chrismas Eve.

I took notes as these women shared the burdens and depressions of their hearts, trying to console each one. Upon arriving for the TV show, I was preceded by an intellectual professor of psychiatry who spoke analytically of the problem of Christmas depression as if it were past tense. He was deep, dull, and remote. When I was asked to make what he had said relevant, I was able to say, "People are depressed right now. Let me give you some current examples of ladies I've spoken with this week." How much more impact we can have on others when we know what's going on *this* week.

The Toastmaster had a fascinating article, "Thank God It's Monday." It stated:

> Perhaps you say, "My brain doesn't start functioning
> in the morning until after my third cup of coffee."
> That's too late. Force your mind to become productive
> as you arise. Your thoughts are important. They don't
> just evaporate like the morning mist. They are with you
> all day long. Be alert. Focus your mind on current
> issues and situations.[1]

Be alert to people of interest in ladies' rooms, at the check-out counter, in airports. Some need your smile, some your hand on a shoulder, some your words of wisdom.

As the C.L.A.S.S. staff and I travel together, I constantly challenge them to keep thinking, to notice people and situations around them. One day Patsy Clairmont met us in San Francisco and could hardly wait to tell us of her adventure on the plane. She was already seated when a couple came on and stopped at her row. They looked at the seat behind Patsy, demanding the lady sitting there to get out since that was their seat assignment. She answered, "No speak English." They yelled at her and still the same answer. The man called for the flight attendant and demanded the lady's removal. She shrugged again unable to understand why everyone was upset with her. Patsy told us that normally she would have ignored the problem but because of our emphasis on being alert to life, she stood up and volunteered to give the couple her seat which had an empty one next to it. The attendant thanked her and the couple sat down.

Patsy noticed the lady's seat belt was not fastened, so she stretched it out to its very fullest and just barely got it shut. Patsy smiled at her and patted her on the hand. A few minutes later the lady reached over, took Patsy's hand in hers, and pressed something into her palm. As Patsy looked she saw a gold chain bracelet and asked, "What's this for?" The lady with a tear in her eye stammered out, "You first American be nice to me." Patsy was touched in telling the incident. She showed us the bracelet and shared the lady's last words to her. "You wear. You remember me?"

That week at C.L.A.S.S. I urged Patsy to relate this tale showing how much of life's flavor we miss when we are not alert to what's going on around us. As you tune in more closely with your surroundings, you will feel your mind moving and your material track expanding.

Another obvious way to fill up the emptiness in our minds is to read everything, everywhere, at all times. If you're in the doctor's office and his magazines are 12 years old, rejoice. You can see firsthand how people were thinking then and compare it with the present for better or for worse.

Read the paper each day. I try to at least glance through the paper before I go out each day. Even if I am teaching a seminar at 9:00 A.M., I see what happened overnight before going. I turn on one of the morning news shows while dressing and have an overview of the world before I leave to speak. It takes so little *time* to be ABOVE AVERAGE. I find people amazed that I, the speaker, have read the paper when they, the audience, are still buttoning their blouses.

As an experiment I took ten *Time* magazine covers with pictures of people sufficiently prominent and current to be known around the world. I held them up in front of the audience and had the women write down the name of each person. Upon correcting the papers, we found that the average member of these ABOVE AVERAGE groups had three out of ten right.

If we leaders don't know what's going on in the world, who does?

Bruce Bawer, English teacher at the State University of New York at Stony Brook, writes in an article entitled, "Ignorance (Not Stupidity) Is Rampant on College Campuses":

College students today are amazingly lacking in important knowledge, and it's no laughing matter.... If I were dealing with simpletons, none of this would bother me profoundly. But my students are not simple-minded. Most get good marks in their major subjects, and many intend careers in medicine, engineering, law. Far from being "slow," they are intelligent, and on their way to becoming the "leaders of tomorrow." But they do not have the knowledge that a college student, let alone a leader, ought to have....

It is up to the individual parent to influence these tastes and interests as positively as possible. For example, buy the kid a few books instead of a video game. Put a globe in his room and look at it with him every now and then. Take him to a symphony concert so that he will be able to appreciate Mozart as well as Meatloaf when he grows up (and recognize the name). Walk him through the local museum on a Saturday afternoon. Keep an atlas, a dictionary, a history book, and a set of encyclopedias around the house, and make conspicuous use of them. Ration the TV. A little imagination on the part of a parent can go a long way toward helping a child learn.

...It is not the most systematic method of education, but it is, at present, the only way to keep the most advanced civilization on earth from producing the most inexcusably ignorant generation of college graduates in its history.[2]

Long before Professor Bawer was teaching, my father had the same idea. He not only read the paper each day but he gave us children capsulized versions of the day's news before we went to school. As I look back on it, I'm sure much of our success was due to his keeping our minds alert to life. During political campaigns he taught us the issues and made us care who won.

I've followed his pattern in raising my children to be alert to the present. This policy takes dedication on our part and a willingness to read, study and digest so that we can disseminate our knowledge attractively enough for our children to listen.

With ignorance being rampant in the world today,

It Takes So Little To Be ABOVE AVERAGE.

13

Journalize for the Future

We have seen the value of recording the past and being alert to the present. Now let's learn how to journalize for the future. As we begin to write down today's thoughts, we record patterns which will help us to understand ourselves in the future.

What is journalizing? In *The Toastmaster* magazine it says, "Unlike a diary a journal is not an hour-by-hour listing of what happens each day, but a recording of thoughts and feelings. It's an unstructured writing out of the events of your life...*as you see them*. It gives you a true perspective of the world and your role in it. A journal, done properly, is an intensely personal experience."[1]

Because journalizing is an intensely personal experience where we openly lay down our inner lives, we need to write in private and keep our thoughts locked up. If we expect others to read our words, we will not be honest. Journalizing is a pouring out of our heart on paper.

How do I start? Get yourself a notebook, sit down and write whatever thoughts go through your head. Robert Johnston says:

> Allow your mind to drift into a centered state of consciousness...relax and let your mind naturally focus or center itself. If you try to focus it, you will spoil it. Trying to concentrate, forcing a focus, or impatience will prevent you from realizing whole mind consciousness and the result will be actualization of only five percent

to 10 percent of your mind. In a relaxed state, allow
your mind to naturally focus itself and you will realize
the other 90 percent to 95 percent of your mind power.[2]

When you're confident no one is going to read your thoughts,
it's amazing how fast they come and how deep they dig.

New York psychologist, Ira Progoff, records his "Intensive Journal" in a looseleaf notebook with twenty-one colored dividers
labeling different topics of his life. The form is not so important
as the feelings. Journalizing becomes therapy for the writer, a time
when you don't have to worry about what other people think of
your ideas. Don't allow grammar, spelling and punctuation to slow
down your thoughts—just pour them out.

What do I say? Some people write as if the words were a letter
to themselves, some as if they were explaining their problems to a
counselor, and some as if they were praying to God. As you focus
your direction, start writing what comes to your mind. You may
think you'll have nothing to say, but our experience tells us that as
a woman sits down to be honest with herself she often writes for
hours. Jerry Labhart of Ft. Worth wrote Francine Jackson about
her first journalizing. "Healing of the memory administered by our
Lord is such a blessing. Your instruction of pouring out my feelings
to God on paper is better than any tranquilizer on the market."

Jerry Mason, in "A Different Way to Pray," began journalizing
to help in his prayer life. He got a notebook, sat down and wrote
six pages of "pent-up prayers":

> I write informally, not to impress but to communicate—
> conveying my heart in a way that works for me, using
> phrases such as these:
>
> —Dear God,
> —Tonight I feel...
> —I want to thank You for...
> —In Your Word You've told me to...
> —I'm not sure I understand...
> —Father, help me to...
> —Today I...
> —I wonder...
>
> and much more.[3]

What good does journalizing do me? Your writing becomes

a personal record of your inner life. As you look back over your thoughts, you will remember how you felt and you will see patterns of behavior which may need to be changed.

Tristine Rainer, author of *The New Diary*, says, "The diary is a never-ending process of search and discovery. It changes as you change; and by acting as a mirror to the self it encourages personal transformation."[4]

James Cummings who has kept a diary since he was thirteen years old writes, "I feel that if you live an interesting life and are aware of it—if you go through each day and then record that day, it becomes a reciprocal process. You're living well to record well, and it goes on and on."[5]

Roseanne Clark wrote me:

> I began my journal the Friday that Francine challenged us to do so. Writing in it has become the highlight of my day (I've written over two hundred pages since C.L.A.S.S.). Some days the words pour from my pen. Others, I have to force myself to write about things which are difficult. In writing about the hard things, I have found answers. I have not only learned to express myself on paper, but I can now verbally express myself to my husband without fear of rejection. I think he must have learned more about who I really am in the last three months than he did in our previous nineteen years of marriage.
>
> My journal has proved on numerous occasions to be a source of encouragement to *me*. At times when I began to go into depression I picked up my journal and read how God had met my need in a similar situation.

One of the unexpected results of journalizing is that the writer learns how to communicate feelings on paper, and then is able to communicate feelings in person.

Roseanne sent us a section of her journal done in her "think spot," a park an hour's drive from her home.

> Lord, suddenly I see my life, not as a mess, but as the background of a child's puzzle—the kind with the outlines of the pieces drawn on it. I see not hundreds of small pieces, but ten (I don't know why that number,

Lord) neatly laid out around the edges. I feel an air of expectancy as if suddenly you are going to pick up each piece and lay them neatly into place. I shed a lot of tears today, Lord, not tears of sadness, or depression, or feeling sorry for myself, but rather tears which just poured from me because of my sense of the overwhelming things You are doing in my life.

As you can see from Roseanne's writing when she puts her thoughts on paper they become a beautiful collection of gems which if strung together would someday become a book. What we don't write down today, we may not remember tomorrow.

Is journalizing scriptural? David was a master journalizer and his psalms are ours today because he took the time to write down his feelings. He talked to God in a personal way and his thoughts then are so like ours today. Look at Psalm 55 for one example. David is afraid for his life and he cries out to God:

> Give ear to my prayer, O God and hide not thyself from my supplication. Attend unto me, and hear me: I mourn in my complaint, and make a noise; because of the voice of the enemy, because of the oppression of the wicked: for they cast iniquity upon me, and in wrath they hate me (verses 1-3).

Have you ever felt like David? Do you ever cry out to the Lord? "Listen God! Listen. Don't hide from me. Where are you when I need you? Can't you hear me crying and complaining? People are talking about me and turning against me. They framed me and now everyone thinks it's my fault and they all hate me."

> My heart is sore pained within me: and the terrors of death are fallen upon me. Fearfulness and trembling are come upon me, and horror hath overwhelmed me (verses 4-5).

"My stomach's in knots, I think I'm dying. I'm scared to death, my hands are shaking, and I feel like the lead in a horror movie."

> And I said, Oh, that I had wings like a dove! for then would I fly away, and be at rest. Lo, then would I wander far off, and remain in the wilderness (verses 6-7).

"Oh God, get me out of here. Let me fly away and have a moment of peace. If only I could get out of these circumstances, I could be happy. Oh God even the desert looks good to me now!"

Don't David's words sound familiar? Don't the words of the past have meaning for the present to help us in the future? If David can do it so can you.

Nancy Williams came to our Dallas C.L.A.S.S., a victim of agoraphobia, the paralyzing fear of being in open spaces. For twenty years she had kept this fear to herself and had only gone out of the house when her husband was with her. She amazed herself when she stood up in the small group and confessed this fear to the other ladies. This outpouring of her heart brought instant support from the other ladies which began a healing. I suggested she start writing down a journal of her feelings as she worked her way out of her phobia. I didn't hear from her, so one day as I was in the Dallas airport I gave her a call to ask how she was doing. She sounded like a different person as she explained, "When you told me to write it all down, I didn't think I could do it, but I sat down with the paper and wrote sentences for six hours. I think I'm writing a book!"

It's amazing what can happen when we sit down with pen in hand and start to write.

Ruth Nichols of Ft. Worth went home from C.L.A.S.S. and sat down to journalize. She took separate pieces of paper and put a heading on each one:

- Things I must do
- Things I need to do
- Things I would like to do
- Things I could do
- Things I enjoy doing
- Things I would be doing if I had the talent, nerve, ability, and/or confidence (my fantasy)
- Things I don't like about myself
- Things I can do to improve myself so I can then be able to help others
- Things I have done that I am proud of
- Things I have done to make money or as a career
- Things I have done or interests I have had over the last three months

After writing the headings she went back to fill in what must be done or what she thought about each topic. By the last page she had thirty-six different items listed.

The definition of "think" is to: devise a plan, form a mental picture of. By journalizing you devise a plan, you commit your feelings down on paper each day. As you review this, you form a mental picture of what your inner life was like at that moment.

So to journalize is to think, planning today to make mental pictures for the future.

Fill your horn with oil and be on your way.[6]

It Takes So Little Today To Be ABOVE AVERAGE Tomorrow.

14

Outline Life

Paul tells us in the Bible that we are to do all things decently and in order and this guideline applies to our creative thinking. If our thoughts are to amount to anything we must train them to move along in some semblance of order. Even creative thinking must have some form or sense of pattern and we *can* change sloppy habits when we see value in a new mind-set.

So far we've been looking at the MATERIAL we gather in our thinking and we've filled our mental file drawers with our reservoir from the PAST, with alertness to life in the PRESENT and with journalizing pages that will help us communicate better in the FUTURE. Now how do we put our thoughts in order. To achieve our goal of thinking ABOVE AVERAGE we must begin to think in outline form. Many people have much material adrift in their heads but don't know how to organize it instantly to make the knowledge useful. "When wise people speak they make knowledge attractive..."[1] Confusion is not an appealing condition, but orderly words are attractive; they make learning easy.

Whether you are ever going to speak, lead or teach, or whether you just want to improve your communication with family and friends, you will profit by learning to think in outline form.

For many of you the mere mention of outlining reminds you of a high school or college composition class where outlining was overwhelming. Some serious teacher intent upon stamping outlines indelibly in each little head, wrote ominous symbols on the blackboard. "Roman numeral I," "capital A," "regular 1," "little a" and so on. You knew you would never have any need for these indented lines so you shut your mind to this lesson. But think again. Now that you're learning to use more than one mental track at a time, you will learn to outline and love it. God has already outlined life for us. In fact, God Himself is a three-point outline: Father, Son, Holy Spirit. He gave order to the universe when He created the earth in seven days and He outlined our year in four seasons—spring, summer, autumn, winter; our calendar into twelve months and our day into twenty-four hours. He arranged our lives into past, present, and future. He made each straight line to have a left, center, and right; positions to be up, down, or sideways; events to be good, bad or indifferent.

These are all outlines and all ones that we have previously memorized. Without any new instruction, we already know nine outlines without using one Roman numeral. God created order and yet so many of our minds are floating in limbo, with thoughts, even inspired thoughts, unattached to any form of organization. Is it not logical that if our minds are fuzzy our daily lives can't be much better? If we wish to be ABOVE AVERAGE, we must train our minds to do what they were originally made for: to think in logical order, to outline life!

Where do we start? Let's use one of the most valuable, simple outlines, sometimes called the "Five Journalistic Ws." Write them on a card and tape it near your phone until you have them memorized. Let's say you call a friend and you get an answering machine. The average person either hangs up quickly or mumbles a few incoherent words, sometimes even forgetting to say who he is. As you train yourself to put life in order, you will use this simple outline:

WHO: This is Joan Collins.

WHAT: Our church is having a supper.

WHERE: In the fellowship hall.

WHEN: On Wednesday at 6:30 P.M.

WHY: To raise money for new kitchen equipment. If you can go, call me back at 792-5416.

When the person comes home and listens to a jumble of messages and blank spaces, yours clearly will stand out like a jewel.

If you are to order something over the phone, you can use this same outline.

WHO: This is Mrs. Paul Stevens.

WHAT: I want to order one pair of Nike tennis shoes, #328, 9B, in blue.

WHERE: Send them to 6 Beechwood Drive, North Haven, Connecticut.

WHEN: As soon as possible.

WHY: I chose to order through you as I've always been satisfied with your quick service.

The order clerk will be thrilled at your concise and positive words.

To communicate a simple message to your family write:

WHO: Fred.

WHAT: I want you to clean

WHERE: Your room and bath

WHEN: This afternoon

WHY: Because we've having company for dinner.

Fred doesn't have to guess about what I want done or when I need it completed or why he's doing it.

Just from these three examples on one basic outline you can see how helpful this system is to pull your thoughts together and keep you from leaving out important details.

Let's work with a convenient three-point outline: past, present, and future. We just used those for our last three chapters: Start with the PAST, Be alert to the PRESENT, Journalize for the FUTURE.

People can remember so much better when ideas are presented in order. When Barbara Bueler, who is now our "outlining expert," was first working with C.L.A.S.S., she went to a retreat at Mt. Herman. At dinner a friend announced, "Barbara is learning how to speak and give talks. Tell us about it Barbara." All eyes turned to Barbara. She swallowed and replied simply, "In the past I used to chatter aimlessly, presently I'm learning all I can about speaking, so that in the future I can share my testimony of hope with others." Barbara was so concise and clear that later several people inquired about her testimony of hope.

So many questions can be answered with the Past, Present, Future Outline.

> "Why are you eating so little?"
> "In the past, I was overweight, so I'm dieting now in order to be thin in the future."

> • • •

> "What are you doing back in school?"
> "Back in the 50s I majored in psychology. I'm now getting an M.A. at Cal State so I can become a marriage counselor in the future.

As you begin to think in outline form your daily communication will improve.

When I discuss marriage problems with a couple I use the Left, Center, Right Outline. "Your marriage started out with both of you in the center, the two became one." I then repeat the problems that have separated them placing one in left field and one in right. I often take two bottles, two pens, two figurines or whatever's handy to represent the two people and move the items around. I show the three alternatives of solving their problem. *She* can go all the way from left field to where he is, expecting nothing in return. *He* can go all the way from right field to her, expecting nothing in return or *they* each can come in from the extremes, compromising and forgiving, until they meet in the center. I show them how the Lord can bring them together when they are willing. "... If I be lifted up... I will draw all men unto me."[2] This outline is so simple yet it keeps us on the track of solving relationship problems and when I move the symbolic couple around they begin to see how far astray they are and what they need to do to come back to center.

One day Barbara was watching football with her husband, John, when she realized the referee spoke in a brief three-point outline.

She mentioned this revelation to John who said, "Oh, no, he says much more than that." Barbara added with joy, "You just wait until the next foul and I'll prove it to you." The foul came and the referee gave his signals as he said: "Illegal holding, #65, 10 yards." Barbara showed John this was a What, Who, and How Outline.

> What: Illegal holding
> Who: #65
> How: By a 10-yard penalty

As Barbara has learned to see all of life in outlines, she even made one up for my birthday. Since our C.L.A.S.S. theme is, "A word fitly spoken is like an apple of gold...," she gave me a candle shaped like an apple and, in addition, Barbara made an acrostic outline from the word "apple":

We thank you for the:

> **A**ppreciation you show us,
> **P**raise you give us,
> **P**runing you do when we need it,
> **L**ove you bestow upon us,
> **E**nduring friendships you have built.

Had she shared these same thoughts without the outline, I would not have remembered them correctly, but by attaching them to a word I knew, she assured my recall.

A few years ago I taught Proverbs 9 as a Bible study. Because I attached it to an appropriate acrostic I still remember it. Proverbs 9 tells what a wise woman is:

> **W**illing
> **I**ntelligent
> **S**table
> **D**ignified
> **O**pen
> **M**ature

Recently Barbara was speaking at a women's retreat. It was time for prayer but Barbara sensed some ladies were afraid to pray. She did a quick message using another simple outline: Problem, Result, Solution.

Problem:	Many women are afraid to pray in public.
Result:	They are full of fear and often stay away.
Solution:	Write a simple outline in your Bible.

As Barbara explained what to write for those who needed help, she noticed they all opened up their Bibles. She had them jot down for future reference these words:

Opening:	Thank you God for this beautiful day.
Petition:	Please bless each lady here.
Closing:	In Jesus name, Amen.

This may sound too simple to you spiritual giants, but it provided a crutch for those who had never dared to pray out loud. They need no longer be afraid.

As some are insecure in how to pray we have found that many women don't write thank-you notes because they don't know what to say. Barbara came up with an easy-to-remember outline:

Personal:	You're special...
Purpose:	Thank you for...
Plan:	Keep in touch.

• • •

Dear Lauren,

You always know just what to get for a present and when I saw your gift at the shower last week, I knew from the tasteful wrapping paper and cluster of violets on the top that I would love what was inside.

When I opened the box and saw the white porcelain bunny with those big eyes and pink ears I was delighted. How thoughtful of you to choose something I can add to my "rabbit collection." Thank you for caring and for coming to the shower.

As soon as Dick and I get settled we'll have you and Randy over for dinner.

> With love and appreciation,
> Judy

Do you see how easy it is to write a personal thank-you note? Whenever someone gives you a gift, they deserve a note of thanks which specifically mentions the item. When they've had you for a special dinner, they deserve a note with a mention of some gourmet dish or the new wallpaper in the foyer. The person receiving the note needs to know that you remember the actual gift or what home you were at. Don't ever send a card that is imprinted with, "Thank you for the gift," unless you also enclose a specific note.

Don't you love to do things for people who thank *you* personally and warmly? To be ABOVE AVERAGE we must always have a grateful spirit for whatever anyone does for us and be sure to let them know it.

It's always special when you get a thank-you note that the person didn't *need* to write. Stormie Omartian came to our C.L.A.S.S. at the Crystal Cathedral. Although she has her own Christian ministry with her husband Michael and has a best-selling album where you exercise to the "Hallelujah Chorus," she took the time to write me this most welcome note.

> Dear Florence, Fred, Marita, and Staff,
> I want to thank you for giving me so much of yourselves during the three days of Basic C.L.A.S.S. in November. The Teaching was a Treasure of Training Touching the heart, Tightening the reins of the mind and Transforming the spirit. (How am I doing?)
> All the material was clear, concise, and valuable. All speakers were *excellent.* I pray that the wealth of your lives continue to enrich millions of others as it has enriched mine.
> Looking forward to seeing you again.
> With much love and blessings,
> Stormie Omartian

One day while in a gift shop I saw a little fish pillow with the words "Body and Sole." Since my friend Johnny Green composed the real *Body and Soul*, I bought the pillow and had it mailed to him. Here's the class thank-you note he sent me:

> Florence, cherished friend:
>
> I got *SUCH* a kick and warm giggle from your "BODY AND *SOLE*" fish! You're pretty darn cute, you are!! How very dear of you, busy as you always are, to think of me and go to the trouble of sending me that adorable "trophy"!! We'll have to find some sort of a special place for "him"—("her"?—"it"?).
>
> I hope that this note finds you, Fred and all those dear to you in topmost form in all departments.
>
> My restated thanks are accompanied by Bonnie's and my........
>
> > Warmest embraces and love.......
>
> John Green

We've seen how a simple outline can help in thank-you notes. Leonara Bianchi from the Walnut Creek C.L.A.S.S. wrote, "Beyond speaking, however, I found that by using your outlining principles as a wonderful tool, my business letters are much more effective."

On an airplane I sat next to John Raynesford, an executive with Atlantic-Richfield. Discussing his fascinating career, he summed up the purpose of his visit to each office: "My job is not to solve problems, but to get problems solved while giving others the credit."

His daily life is a two-point outline: Problem-Solution. This same outline will help you deal with your own problem situations. Let's use a three-point outline, however: Problem, Alternative, Solution. Your daughter didn't make the cheerleading squad and she is crying over it. Discuss the **Problem** and be sympathetic. Go over the attitude **Alternatives**:

1. Stay miserable and let everyone know you're a poor sport.
2. Lie and say you didn't want to be on the stupid squad anyway.

3.   Admit you're disappointed but accept it as a growth experience.

As you discuss the *Alternatives*, guide her into choosing the *Solution*.

You go to the Church Women's Board Meeting and they find there is a deficit. You speak up and say, "Our *Problem* is lack of money. Here are some *Alternatives*: 1. We can each chip in $100; 2. We can have a rummage sale; or 3. We can hold a spring luncheon and fashion show. Let's vote on a *Solution*." You are instantly brilliant. You've been able to take a problem, present alternatives, and show them how to choose a solution. It takes so little to be ABOVE AVERAGE!

In the last chapter of *Blow Away the Black Clouds,* I show how to use alternatives in counseling. The understanding of this simple approach will make any one of you able to listen to someone's *Problem*, show them *Alternatives*, and guide them into choosing the correct *Solution*.

When I spoke at the School of Prophets at First Baptist of Dallas, I heard Dr. W.A. Criswell use a two-point outline that was easy to remember: PASTOR and PEOPLE. He gave many excellent examples of how each church needs a PASTOR and PEOPLE. Because his outline was simple and clear I still remember the message and this one example in particular:

If the PASTOR says he needs $12.55
the PEOPLE say the PASTOR has money on his mind.
If the PASTOR says he needs $14 million,
the PEOPLE say the PASTOR has vision.

Are you beginning to see the value of using outlines in life? God set the world in order and He so *wants* us to follow in His footsteps. We've looked at outlining some messages, product orders, notes to children, marriage problems, football games, Bible study, prayers, thank-you notes, business meetings, counseling, and sermons. Do you see how clear life can be when we think in outline form?

It Take So Little To Be ABOVE AVERAGE.

15

Practice Your Scales

Now that we've seen the value of thinking in an orderly fashion, let's practice. Barbara Bueler calls outlining the "scales of communication." The more hours you practice your scales, the better you will be at the recital.

Sheila Wicks of Ft. Worth wrote after attending C.L.A.S.S.:

> Friday morning when Barbara shared on outlining it
> was all I could do not to stand up and shout. I too had
> a mental block about outlining from my high school
> years. A light turned on and I realized in so many areas
> I was already using outlines. For the rest of the seminar
> I was like a sponge in every area.

Let's all be like sponges and soak up outlines everywhere we look and listen. Magazine and TV ads are the most obvious material to work with because they have to say a lot in a brief space or time.

A new Hilton ad is an obvious two-point outline:
>   YES we did (change our decor)
>   NO we didn't (change our service)

An ad for Bell System Calling Card tells:
>   How it works
>   How to get yours

The advertisement for the Ramada Renaissance:
> You deserve it
> You can afford it

Pitney-Bowes Dictaphone:

B.D.	A.D.
(Before Dictaphone)	(After Dictaphone)

Stanford University Nursing Center:
> Nursing touches you with hands that:
>> Care
>> Lead
>> Teach
>> Touch

How to stop smoking:
> Here's how
> Here's why
> What you'll get
> Where
> When

Do you see how easy it is to spot ready-made outlines in ads? Soon you'll be outlining all of life and communicating clearly. *United* magazine had a glossy spread of pictures showing attractive table settings. The headlines by each picture became the outline:
DINNER
> —on the porch
> —on the deck
> —by the pool
> —in the yard
> —on the terrace[1]

Brochures frequently have obvious outlines:
> International Prayer Fellowship:
>> Where we began...
>> Where we are...
>> Where we've been...
>> Where we're going...
> Arizona Women's Retreat:
>> Receive
>> Reflect
>> Rejoice

Using Air Wisconsin is as easy as:
    1...
       2...
          3...

As you do your scales by outlining ads, brochures, menus (breakfast, lunch and dinner), and billboards, you become aware of how much of life is in order.

In *Time*, Hugh Sidey said of the state of the union message:

> It is overhyped by presidents, overanticipated by citizens, and overwhelmed by TV."[2]

An article on John Kennedy reported his being asked, "Do you like being president?" He supposedly answered:

> I have a nice house.
> The pay is good.
> I can walk to work.[3]

Reviews are fun to read. One on a theatrical production on Broadway in New York said of Doug Henning, star of *Magic Show*, "There are three things he cannot do on stage: sing, dance, and act."[4]

As your eye begins to see outlines, your ear will begin to hear them. A TV evangelist said, "We must figure out who we are, what we're doing, and where we're going."

Bo Gritz, Missing in Action (M.I.A.) rescuer, on an early morning TV show said, "We must solidify our efforts, evaluate our progress, and liberate our prisoners."

Start listening to your pastor with an ear newly-tuned and write down his sermon outline. If he doesn't appear to have one, you make one up. I still outline every sermon or speech for practice.

Now you are ready to outline Bible verses for your own edification and for teaching others more clearly. Jesus said:

In John 14:6:	In John 15:
"I am the way	"I am the vine,
the truth	You are the branches...,
and the life."	My father is the gardener."

In Acts 2:42:
The early church
learned from the apostles
fellowshipped together,
shared meals together,
and prayed.

In Acts 6:7:
The word of God continued
  to spread.
The number of disciples grew
  larger.
A great number of priests
  accepted the faith.

In Acts 18:8:
Many people in Corinth
heard the message,
believed and were baptized.

In 1 Corinthians 3:6:
I planted the seed,
Apollos watered the plant,
God gave the increase.

In Romans 8:28:
All things work together for
  good for those
who love the Lord,
who are called according
  to His purpose.

In Philippians 3:10:
All I want is to
know Christ,
feel the power of his
  resurrection,
share in His sufferings,
become like Him.

In Ephesians 6:10-17:
Put on the armor of God,
Have truth for a belt,
Put on righteousness for your
  breastplate,
Add readiness as shoes,
Carry faith as a shield,
Accept salvation as a helmet,
Use the word of God as the
  sword.

In 1 Peter 5:2-3:
Church leaders should
be shepherds of the flock,
look after it willingly,
work from a desire to serve,
be examples to the flock.

Do you see how much fun it is to outline Bible verses? After you have done your scales on verses, you can move on to chapters and whole books. I have done the chapter and book of Philemon as a human relations lesson entitled, "How To Win Friends and Influence People."[5]

I show how Paul, who did not have innate charm or tact, handled a personality problem by:

compliments	choice
concern	challenge
congratulations	confidence
compromise	conclusion

I have always forced myself to write out an outline and print up copies of every Bible study I've ever done. I am so grateful now that I did this since I have boxes of outlines to draw from in speaking and writing.

Remember when you teach Bible studies, realize how important it is for you to outline your message,

so *you* will *know* what you're saying;
so *they* will be able to *remember* it.

As your mind begins to think in outline form, you will speak and write better and your new order will pervade the family. Patsy Clairmont, our court jester, shares that when she first heard me outlining menus while out to dinner she didn't know an outline from an outlaw from an outhouse! But as she has done her practicing, outlining *has* become a part of her family life. One morning Patsy heard a knock at the door. She opened it and there stood 7-year-old Jason.

"What are you doing home?" she asked in surprise.

"I've quit school."

"You've quit school? What brought you to that decision?"

Jason looked up and stated clearly,

"It's too long,
It's too hard,
It's too boring."

Patsy was thrilled and said, "Jason, you've done a three-point outline!" then added, "You've just described life. Get on the bus."

How much more interesting it is to read the paper when you are spotting outlines on every page. One of our C.L.A.S.S. participants gave our staff a toast: "You are all:

Proud
Professional
Prepared
Positive

Debbie Laurie sent this letter showing us how she had applied the principles of outlining to everyday life.

> Dear Florence,
>
> You're right. Our ministry begins first at home. After C.L.A.S.S., I began to think, how can I motivate my nine- and twelve-year-old daughters to become organized in the morning? Below is my three-point outline:
>
> A. Bath
>   1. Toilet
>   2. Teeth
>   3. Tresses
> B. Bedroom
>   1. Sheets
>   2. Slacks
>   3. Shoes
> C. Breakfast
>   1. Bread
>   2. Bacon
>   3. Banana
>
> Oh, this is so much fun! Thank you, thank you thank you!

When in San Antonio we trained some new staff, one of these women wrote this outlined thank-you note:

> Dearest Florence and Staff,
>
> Please receive my deepest gratitude for the opportunity you gave me this weekend. 1. It has been a privilege to *watch* you, *work* with you, and *wonder* at all God does through you. 2. I wanted you each to know that I thank you for...
>
> > *risking* your
> >   *reputation,* in allowing us to
> >   *represent* you, C.L.A.S.S. and our Lord.
> > I have *received*
> >   the *rewards.*
>
> 3. I also *recognize* that in your teaching us to be effective leaders and speakers, you have taught us to be like Christ. Because who else is the Great

Communicator? 4. Thank you for the precious ***remembrance*** of God's love from each of you.

Speaking in Him,
Joy Chambers

Let's communicate God's love in such a way that everyone will remember what we say.

It Takes So Little To Be ABOVE AVERAGE.

16

Give Your Brain an Assignment

As I was preparing to lead my first speaking seminar, I tried to break down my speaking into teachable units which I could then communicate to others. As I prayed over the potential outline I came up with these principles:

> Establish need
> Give testimony
> Present a plan
> Offer hope
> Call for commitment
> Expect results

These points expressed how I construct a message with heart, but I then needed Scripture to back up my principles. That night I went to bed and prayed as I often do, "Dear Lord, here's another outline. I need Scripture to go with this. Please give me an answer by morning. I claim your Psalm 31:2, 'Bow down thine ear to me; deliver me speedily...'. In your precious name, Amen."

When I awoke in the morning, my mind was saying, "2 Timothy, 2 Timothy, 2 Timothy." Picking up my Bible and pad of paper and before getting out of bed, I had related the whole book of 2 Timothy to my outline.

I soon realized that much of the material for C.L.A.S.S. came from overnight assignments where I needed to be delivered "speedily." Francine later named it "Give your brain an assignment."

George Ball, corporate executive officer of Prudential-Bache Securities, gives his brain frequent assignments:

> I set aside time to think twice a day. First, early in the morning when I am still at home and before my family is up, I set aside 10-15 minutes for undisciplined, free-wheeling thought—whether it's about the state of the universe or the state of my fountain pen. When I am headed home from work I try to have 15 minutes or so for idea-gathering. At the end of the day one is less fresh and therefore less creative. But I try to put together the ideas I want to concentrate subliminally on overnight and think about the next morning.[1]

Edward Hennessy, Jr., chairman of Allied Corporation, in the same article said:

> I absolutely have had good business ideas come to me in a flash—most often at 2 or 3 A.M. I keep a small flashlight and a pad and pencil by my bed so I can record those thoughts and see if they're as brilliant in the morning light as they seem to be in the wee hours.[2]

As we started teaching others to give their brains assignments, we came up with results far beyond our expectations. Ladies would come in the following morning crying, "It worked! It worked!" One woman was in tears as she said, "This is the first time in my life I've seen evidence that God's real." One beautiful but sad young lady had been unable to apply this principle throughout the seminar. Following our suggestions, the next morning she came in transformed. "I told my brain to give me a verse that would help my depression. I woke up with John 16:24 on my mind and opened the Bible to find, 'Hitherto have ye asked nothing in my name: ask, and ye shall receive, that your joy may be full.' "

Another girl came in looking tired and asked, "How many nights does it take before you can sleep? I gave my brain an assignment and woke up every two hours to see if I had an answer."

A lady said, "I felt foolish putting paper and pen by my bed, but I did it anyway and I woke up with a three-point outline."

Because of the positive results of our brain assignments, I wrote some directions:

1. Believe it will work.
2. Put out paper, pen, and Bible by your bed.
3. Give your brain an assignment.
4. Ask God to answer you "speedily."
5. Write down your first thoughts when you wake up.
6. Thank the Lord for his quick response.

One day as we were talking about the exciting results of "brain assignments," a woman came up with a perfect verse: "I will bless the Lord who has counseled me; Indeed, my mind instructs me in the night" (Psalm 16:7 NASB).

Why waste your night? Our bodies need rest but that 90% of our unused mind is happy to work for us into the wee hours of the morning. Start giving your brain assignments and let the Lord instruct you in the night.

It Takes So Little To Be ABOVE AVERAGE.

C

It Takes So Little
To Look Above Average

17

Have the Attitude of a Servant

It is encouraging that the Bible tells us, "Man looketh on the outward appearance, but the Lord looketh on the heart" (1 Samuel 16:7). Unfortunately we are dealing with human beings here on earth and they do make judgments as soon as they take a look at us. You've often heard, "You never get a second chance to make a good first impression," and that is so true. We would like to think that as Christians how we appear doesn't matter, that everyone sees us through spiritual eyes.

Think for a moment. Is there someone you know whose attitude you don't like? She just walks in the room and you cringe. She doesn't have to open her mouth for just her glance in your direction shows an unacceptable attitude.

Do you have a friend who's always condemning herself? "My house is too small. I'm so depressed." She slumps on the sofa and sighs. You say to yourself, "Shape up! Stand tall! Start moving!" Her lack of bearing bothers you.

Picture now someone who doesn't know how to dress. When your group is going to get together, you wonder what Wanda will wear tonight—will she look even worse than last time? She's probably got a good heart, but who will ever get to know.

If you have been able to think of even one person who fits the above descriptions, you *do* make inner opinions on outside appearances.

You ask, "But doesn't everyone?" Yes, everyone does. That's

why we must pay attention to the basics, the ABCs of leadership.

- ★ Attitude
- ★ Bearing
- ★ Clothing

If we notice others, they are probably noticing us. They might judge us on our externals before they ever get to our heart. We see people and instantly we communicate to our brain what we think of them.

Even if we are so deep that we don't judge a book by its cover, we can't count on many other people having this ability. If we wish to be effective communicators, we must consider our outward appearance, for how we look speaks louder than how we actually may be.

The *A* of our ABCs is *attitude.* Before we open our mouths, people can sense our attitude. If we are haughty, critical, or bored, it shows and when we try to hide our true feelings, people can tell we are phonies. When our inner attitude is one of loving concern, we don't have to hand out lollipops to communicate our generous spirit.

Recently Great Britain had a memorable election, the most impressive electoral sweep of any political party since 1945. Margaret Thatcher said, "It was a larger victory than I had dared hope for."[1] How did Mrs. Thatcher do it? Even though many of her policies are unpopular, she won by being sincerely herself. She has the attitude of a servant, the bearing of a queen, and the clothes of a leader. Margaret, who grew up living behind her father's store as I did, has worked her way up to the top. She has given Britain dignity, and she believes, "All power is a trust. We have to use our power wisely and well." *Time* said of her:

> The Prime Minister was reelected last week not so much because of specific policies as because of her attitudes. Britons at this point seem to care more about having a strong leader then about exactly where they are led.[2]

What a beautiful statement. What an aim for each one of us, to be chosen because of our attitude, because others can tell when they look at us that we have the ABCs of leadership.

What kind of an attitude appeals to others? When we think of becoming a leader, an administrator, a club president, a chairman, or endeavoring to be a good parent, we too often focus on the control, the in-charge feeling. We've often heard, "If I were in charge of this group, we'd get something done," or "When I was president I ran a tight ship." Is leadership "doing and running" or is it, as with Mrs. Thatcher, the right attitude?

When I went in as president of the Women's Club of San Bernardino, I was feared as a religious fanatic by a fringe of the group. Some were afraid I was going to preach or make them join some mystic group. As I prayed about my direction, the Lord led me to 1 Kings 12:7. Solomon had died and his son Rehoboam was about to be crowned king. He went to his father's advisors, asking what he should do to be an effective ruler. They gave him advice which set the attitude for action in my area of leadership:

> Answer all who ask you;
> Speak kindly to all;
> Have the attitude of a servant.

Even though Rehoboam ignored this advice, I followed it.

Prayerfully, I planned my presidency with the aim of answering all who asked, of pleasing each member in every way I could. I spoke kindly to all. I developed an attitude of a servant. As the members realized I was always available, I'd go to their church luncheons, help in the club kitchen, look at their grandchildren's pictures, or visit them in the hospital, they relaxed and became my friends. When I was nominated for a second term, I won as Mrs. Thatcher had, not for my specific policies but for my attitude. One lady said, "You love us all and I never saw you get upset with anyone." True leaders will have the attitude of a servant and speak kindly to all.

It Takes So Little To Be ABOVE AVERAGE.

18

Have the Bearing of a Queen

People love royalty. They want to look up to someone. They want an example to follow. When Jimmy Carter went into office, he misread the American public and thought they wanted a leader who was "one of the gang." He emphasized the ordinary, surrounded himself with down-home buddies and carried his own luggage. Surely there's nothing wrong with doing any of these things, but somehow he didn't come across as presidential. A flurry of articles came out on the qualities of a leader and we all began to ask ourselves what it was we wanted in a president. When given a new choice, we voted for an actor who had practiced for the presidential role and who surely looks the part. When President Reagan is asked a question on a TV press conference he stands up straight, gives a confident smile, and says, "I'm glad you asked that question." He may not know the answer, but he knows his ABCs of leadership. He has the bearing of a king. As you develop your leadership skills, don't let your Christian humility keep you bowed down in the corner. Stand up straight, walk with confidence, speak with conviction.

Frequently, as I converse with the man next to me on an airplane, he will ask, "What's your business?" I reply, "I'm a Christian speaker."

There is always a pause before, "You don't look like a Christian speaker."

"What does a Christian speaker look like?"

"Well, sort of old and dull, black clothes, hair pulled straight back no makeup, carrying a Bible and just home from Africa."

Isn't it a shame we Christian women have the reputation of being evangelical frumps? Let's change that image and develop the bearing of a queen.

As you stand, regally before the mirror of life, pretend there's a string on the top of your head being pulled up to heaven. Keep your elbows back and your tummy pulled in. As a queen, don't look down on the dummies, rather smile on the saints.

A leader must have a beautiful bearing, a look of confidence. Make sure before presenting yourself to the court you're put together in such a secure way that you have no doubts draining your demeanor. What happens when you've left home with a button missing from your left sleeve? All day you keep your left hand behind your back, and don't dare reach for the coffee. What if there's a run in your pantyhose but you're in a hurry and you hope no one will notice. All day you keep standing in corners with your leg against the wall and when you leave rooms you back out. How nervous will you be if you tie a string around a too long slip and hope the lace won't show? You'll keep looking for mirrors to check your hem and you'll have a few friends watching for the fall.

When we are insecure on how we're put together, we waste a whole mental track on worry. We can't have the bearing of a queen when we wonder if our subjects will notice:

We've lost our buttons,
We're running in the wrong direction, and
We're held together by string.

For a regal radiance set your royal train on the right track.

It Takes So Little To Reign ABOVE AVERAGE.

19

Have the Clothing of a Leader

The Bible tells us our beauty should not depend upon our outward adornment. And yet the virtuous woman of Proverbs 31 was clothed in tapestries of scarlet and in purple silks. She had that look of quiet elegance befitting a queen. How about us?

A lady at our Laguna Beach C.L.A.S.S. said, "I always knew I didn't dress well, but I didn't care. After this week, I still know I don't dress well, but now I care." Caring is halfway there.

Does it matter what a Chrisian leader wears? There's no uniform for leadership or requirement for the navy blue blazer that the "dress for success" look suggests. Yet we should always aim to be one step ABOVE AVERAGE. We don't want to be overdone, but we want to set the pace. When I was president of the League of Women Voters, the level of dress for the meetings and teas was tweed suits and flat shoes. They all looked as if they'd been out tramping through the moors in Scotland. I could have headed for the herringbones, but instead I continued to wear my more feminine suits and dresses. Slowly the other women began to change and by the end of the term everyone came dressed up.

Francine Jackson attends Toastmasters in Evergreen, Colorado, the mountain community where she lives. Francine always dresses tastefully in simple elegance even in the mountains. When she first began attending meetings, the women were in jeans and hiking boots, the men in flannel shirts. Called upon to speak on some topic she felt strongly about, Francine titled her message,

"Let's Dress Up." From that time on she noticed a difference in how they all looked and now they do "dress up." Given a living example, people will rise to be ABOVE AVERAGE.

Your aim should be to have a unified or "put together" look. The viewer should see you and not your clothes. One night we took some C.L.A.S.S. ladies to a department store known for its classy clothes at budget prices. We found one dress that was a perfect *bad* example. The background was black and white zebra stripes and right across the bosom was a large zebra head with an open mouth and big eyes. It looked right out of the ark! Scattered across the stripes, here and there, were large flowers in bright orange and hot pink and to give the final touch it had rhinestone buttons.

Since I will give a mini-seminar anywhere, I called the girls over and showed them how not to dress as a leader. Francine found some other bad examples and we held each one in front of us and asked, "When you look at me, what do you see? If the answer is zebras, stripes, or flowers we must be a little too loud."

Try on your clothes and ask yourself, "What do I see?" If you have an outfit that compliments your natural color, if no part of it stands out and your shoes blend with the total look, you are probably all right.

Each one of us is different and we should aim to wear the colors and styles that do the very best for us, not ones that looked good on our friends.

When God appointed Aaron to be the high priest, the spiritual leader, He said, "Make special clothes for Aaron to indicate his separation; beautiful garments that will lend dignity to his work" (Exodus 28:2 TLB). Begin to build a wardrobe of special clothes that will add dignity to your work.

The ABCs of leadership give us some simple guidelines. Have the:

> Attitude of a servant
> Bearing of a queen
> Clothing of a leader

The following letter sums up the attributes of leadership:

Dear Florence,
> I attended your C.L.A.S.S. seminar in Detroit on

February 8-10, 1983. I found it to be entertaining and informative. I was challenged in many areas. I felt better about myself as I left the seminar.

I learned one very important lesson in an area I have struggled with for years. The prim and proper person was always someone I resented. I had a built in prejudice against them. I felt the walls coming down each day I was around you. On Thursday when you explained the importance of always maintaining a servant spirit, I knew you meant it because the night before at the restaurant you had exhibited just that as you took time at our table answering our questions and sharing with us. I couldn't believe a person of your status was spending all that time with us.

As I thought about your ABCs of becoming a quality leader/speaker, I realized my thoughts had changed.

When you said "A" was attitude, I at first felt it was an attitude that creates an *air* of snobbishness. Now I see it as an attitude that creates an *atmosphere* of love.

When you said "B" was for bearing, I saw a bearing determined to *brag* about self. Now I see bearing as determined to *boast* only of Christ.

When you said "C" was for clothing, I saw clothing which exhibited *conceit* over my importance. Now I see it as clothing that exhibits *confidence* in the God we serve.

Thank you for helping to remove my prejudices. I will begin to work on the "so little it takes to be above average." Thank you for following through on a vision that will help those desiring to improve their speaking in order that the gospel be presented with the highest quality possible.

Love,
Dana Ryan

When you act like a leader, walk like a leader, and look like a leader, people will follow you.

It Takes So Little To Be ABOVE AVERAGE.

D

It Takes So Little
To Lead Above Average

20

Give an Announcement

Dull announcements following each other in single file have led many women's clubs over the cliff of monotony into the valley of poor attendance. Unfortunately, once a club is in the valley, it is difficult to renew its membership. In order to keep a women's group alive, those who feel led to make announcements should first ask themselves two questions:

- "What am I trying to say?"
- "Does anyone need to hear it?"

If no further instructions were given, the first question would eliminate the ennui felt when chairmen stumble up totally unprepared, shuffle through stacks of papers, and end up reviewing what everyone wore at the literature section for lack of message. Even if there is something to say, the chairman should ask herself if anyone needs to hear it. If a chairman has objectively answered "yes" to these two questions, she should proceed to the "Four Commandments of Announcements":

1. Make it CLEAR.
2. Make it POSITIVE.

3. Make it BRIEF.
4. Make it COMPLIMENTARY.

Make it clear: Many times a chairman muddles through her announcement and mutters her words in such a way that no one is quite sure what she was talking about by the time she sits down. This confusion promotes murmuring in the ranks and the president can hardly regain control as the debate goes on. "Was it for Tuesday or Wednesday?"; "January or February?"; "Was the money for scholarships or tea chairs?" The simple solution for clear annnouncements is to follow the "Five Journalistic Ws": Who, What, When, Where, and Why.

Who is sponsoring the activity?
What is its plan and purpose?
When is it being held?
Where will it be?
Why is it important to attend?

For example:

WHO:	The Bible study section led by Mrs. Eason is
WHAT:	having an open meeting for all club members
WHEN:	on Thursday morning at 9:30 A.M.
WHERE:	here in the clubhouse.
WHY:	Mrs. Eason will teach the Book of Philippians and cover a subject we all need to hear, "How To Have Joy in Adverse Circumstances."

• • •

WHO:	The Scholarship Committee, chaired by Hazelle Howard
WHAT:	will put on the 18th Annual Scholarship Luncheon
WHEN:	on Wednesday, February 18, at 12:00 noon
WHERE:	at the Arrowhead Country Club.
WHY:	The proceeds will go to nursing students at

Valley College. Knowing the need there is for qualified nurses, I am sure you will want to support this event.

When you have to make an announcement answer the five Ws, leave nothing out, and make it clear.

Make it positive: It is very difficult to instill enthusiasm for any activity if the speaker is dwelling on the negatives: "There's very little to say about next month's speaker"; "I'm new in this job and last year's chairman didn't give me a thing to go on"; "With all the problems I've had dumped on me, there's no way I could do this job right"; "No one in this club has ever had any interest in mental health." After opening lines like these, the chairman would have a difficult time finding volunteers to help. This rejection proves that her position is hopeless so she retreats into obscurity until next month, emerging to try hopelessly again. Whatever your announcement is about, make it positive. If there is nothing good to say about your program perhaps it should be disbanded. On the other hand, an enthusiastic approach, plus some free food, may be all mental health needs to get rolling:

This is my first year as chairman of mental health and I am sincerely challenged by the needs in this community. I have prepared a list of available opportunities for volunteer help and I will present these openings for assistance at my home next Tuesday at noon. I will be serving a chicken salad luncheon with chocolate cream pie for dessert. Now will all of you interested in joining my committee please raise your hands so I'll know how much lunch to prepare?

When I was membership chairman of the League of Women Voters, I asked a lady who owned a beautiful home overlooking a lake if we could use her home for the membership tea. After I announced that the tea would be held at a home everyone had always wanted to see, one of the largest crowds ever attending a membership tea turned out.

Be creative in thinking and be positive in your announcements.

Make it brief: While some members will not stand up to second a motion, there are always plenty of announcers who tend to ramble on. The topic of the garden chairman's report is lost in a torrent of trivia: "You'll never know what trouble I had to go to for these flowers on the tea table today. I started a month ago by calling Helen. She's the one that lives on Lorna Lane next door to Dr. Abbott. She has 200 camellia bushes and anyone would think...." At this point the audience is lost, many are asleep, and several have turned off their hearing aids. Keep their interest by keeping it brief.

Make it complimentary: Many chairmen tend to hide their own insecurities by shifting the blame for potential failure onto other people: "If only I had a decent committee we might accomplish something"; "The district chairman never sent me so much as a postcard"; "When I was president things were really organized, but now..."; "After what happened to this chairmanship last year, it will be a miracle if I can pull this thing together at all."

When I was president of our local women's club, the magazine chairman stood up to give her report. To win district acclamation she needed 100% subscriptions to the national journal so she devised a way to achieve these results. She began by reading off a list of names and asking all those mentioned to stand up. Each lady when called upon stood up, smiled, and turned from side to side so all could see her. When the whole list had been read, the chairman asked everyone to look at them. In the midst of this mystery adulation the chairman stated clearly, "These ladies you are looking at are the only ones in the club who have not renewed their subscriptions and are keeping this club from a district award."

The group sank instantly and gasped in unison. The ladies were insulted with the whole club indignant. The chairman got her 100%, but she was never nominated for any position ever again!

Don't make any negative remarks even if you think they're cute. Keep your comments positive and complimentary. From these narrations of the negatives, it is easy to conclude that if an announcement is worth making at all, it should be clear and to the point. It should be given with a bright, positive enthusiasm. It should be brief and include no chronicle of personal problems, and it should never insult another person, but be complimentary.

If each chairman could be coached to follow these instructions, every women's group would have such pleasant, positive people that many more people would want to join!

It Takes So Little To Be ABOVE AVERAGE.

21

A Proper Introduction

One of the most pathetic of the platform presentations is the introduction of the guest speaker. I have been presented with lengthy lists of everything I've ever done in my life or, at the other end of the scale, I've heard, "There is so much to say about Florence Littauer that I'm not going to say anything. So here she is." The long list puts them to sleep before the speaker gets up and the "here she is" makes them wonder if there was, in fact, *anything* to say about her.

One night I was scheduled to speak at a mother-daughter banquet held in a long room about the size of two bowling alleys. On one side was a folding plastic wall and on the far side of that was a strolling mariachi band in full swing. As the audience arrived I discovered few mothers had come, just the girls and grandmothers. I looked around for the microphone and there was none. Realizing there was no way these elderly ladies could hear me over the band without a mike, I asked the chairman if I could stand halfway down the side of the room. When it was time for me to speak the chairman announced, "Our speaker tonight does not want to stand here by the head table where a normal speaker would stand. She's down there somewhere in the middle of you all. Oh yes, there she is." She waved her hand toward me and sat down without having even given my name. I waited in amazement for the introduction but she rose up slightly from her chair and called out, "Well, get on with it."

By this introduction she communicated clearly that I was not normal, I had strange ideas, I had been at least momentarily lost, my talk would be a chore to listen to, and my name was not significant enough to mention.

How much worse could she have done? Could she learn how to introduce a speaker? In C.L.A.S.S. we have a popular section on introductions and so many ladies say they will never be afraid of this assignment again. In fact, we encourage our graduates to volunteer to introduce guests in their clubs or churches to spare the speaker an awkward start.

I once spoke at the same conference as Dr. E.V. Hill, the black evangelist. Before Dr. Hill spoke a well-meaning man, wanting to let the audience know each speaker had been assigned a "shepherd," in humor announced, "This week in honor of Dr. Hill we will reinstitute slavery." No one thought this quip was funny.

Oh how we need people who can correctly introduce a speaker. Although professional speakers will usually have a prepared introduction which they request you read with enthusiasm, the average local speaker will rely on you to come up with something to say. What should you do?

Few people look upon the introduction with significance and yet it serves a vital purpose. Picture the speaker sitting on the stage waiting to be introduced. We will assume she is unknown to the group. The ladies at the luncheon have already prejudged her. Those who assume they are arbiters of proper attire have decided she is not stylishly dressed and is probably too religious. The spiritual giants of the group have noticed the speaker is wearing eye makeup and therefore is probably not even a Christian. The intellectuals think she hasn't passed the seventh grade and the insecure see her as intimidating because she carries a briefcase. These conflicting thoughts fill the air and build an invisible wall between the audience and the speaker, who may never be able to break it down.

The purpose of an introduction is to "break down the middle wall of partition between us" (Ephesians 2:14). These brief moments should be prepared carefully to achieve this desired result, to "break down the wall" between the speaker and the audience. Think of yourself as the connecting link between the two, as a bridge from the mouth of the speaker to the mind of the hearer.

The preparation. You should present enough information to establish credentials, show why the speaker is gifted on his subject, and give the audience a reason to listen. Don't read an endless list of schools attended, and be sure you don't give away the plot of the message. Picture what it does to me when the introducer says, "Florence's wedding was in *Life* magazine and later both her sons were born with brain damage."

There goes the fun and the trauma right out of my talk. Why not let the introducer give the whole speech—if she has already given away the heart of the message. Don't turn the introduction into a speech of your own and don't get off the track.

The plan. In order to make an effective presentation you should answer for the audience the following questions: Who? Where? What? and Why?

As an example—the audience needs to know the speaker's name—and be sure you pronounce it properly; ***where*** he or she is from; ***what*** talents, abilities, or credits he or she has that somewhat pertain to today's group and topic; and ***why*** this person was chosen to speak for this occasion.

Remembering these four simple words—Who, Where, What, and Why—can give you the ability to quickly interview anyone at any time and come up with an appropriate introduction. By adding the one word "When" to your format you will have the formula for writing information for publicity, posters, newspaper articles, radio, and TV announcements.

The presentation. When it is time for the introduction, walk confidently to the podium. Try to do your part without notes, if possible, and keep your purpose in mind: break down that middle wall of partition between us. Be brief and enthusiastic. Be interesting and positive. Don't give away the plot. While most introducers are not engaging enough, a few go overboard in their praise of the speaker. Occasionally, I'll have some bubbly lady tell the audience that I'm a cross between Erma Bombeck and Phyllis Diller and that I'll keep them in stitches. This oversell causes those who didn't want to be there in the first place to glare at me and send messages like, "You just try to make us laugh."

From here on you will enjoy evaluating those who introduce others and you will learn from both their strengths and weaknesses. When someone asks, "Who will introduce the speaker?" please volunteer.

For those of you who are saying to yourselves right now, "If she thinks I'm getting up on a stage she's crazy," let me point out how important it is to be able to introduce a person correctly in social situations. So many people are so insecure with introductions that they tend to ignore a new person or neglect a friend who is new to the group. Whether or not your neighbor wants to return next week to the Bible study may depend upon how well you introduce her this week:

> This is my friend Sally who just moved here from Chicago. She works part time as a nurse at the local hospital and her hobby is raising African violets. She came today to meet new people and I know you'll all enjoy getting acquainted with Sally.

People who once passed through Chicago, ever went to a hospital, or own a single African violet will have a basis for conversation because of your bright and brief introduction.

Memorize *Who, Where, What,* and *Why* and with these four words you'll be able to introduce anyone, anywhere, at any time.

It Takes So Little To Be ABOVE AVERAGE.

22

Preside Over the Meeting

Whenever pollsters survey Americans' fears they always find that "standing in front of a group" is number one on their list. We are all so afraid of being either laughed at or looking foolish in front of others that we prefer not to try at all. Jim Newman, a fellow member of the National Speaker's Association, in his new book, *Release Your Brakes*, explains the feelings people have when faced with even a supportive audience:

> When a person first joins Toastmasters, the pressure of standing in front of a few friendly, encouraging people can be pretty heavy. Some will find very creative reasons for not being able to come back and others will return and further develop their skills.
>
> Those who return probably have no more potential, but they are responding to the pressure in a very different way. When you see an outstanding speaker performing with great enthusiasm and confidence, you can be sure that he has been subjected to the same pressures that have been felt by every other public speaker. He has not gritted his teeth and forced himself to continue.... Instead, he has formed the habit of responding to the successively higher levels of pressure in a positive way, using them as turn-ons instead of tie-ups.[1]

What will you do when asked to be president of the women's club or chairman of the Prudish Priscilla Circle? Will you, like Moses, say, "Who me? I am slow of tongue," or will you realize God has prepared you for such a time as this. So few women have any idea of how to run a meeting that you will appear brilliant if you say, "Will the opening meeting of the Choir Robe Committee come to order." Take whatever opportunity presents itself and become a leader. It Takes So Little To Be ABOVE AVERAGE.

Purpose: Every group needs a leader and we will assume that it is YOU! Begin by finding out what the purpose of your group is and what its chief function is to be. As you ask the past president, the pastor, and the people what the purpose is, you may be amused at the conflicting answers and instantly see why this group hasn't gone very far in the past.

So few leaders take the time or effort to find out what the purpose of the flock is and bumble through half the year before finding out no one knows where they're going. If there is no true goal, either think one up or disband the group.

As soon as you have a goal in mind, try to state it in a simple and, if possible, catchy way and repeat it often to the group. They will feel so much more comfortable when they know why they are meeting, and repetition is essential. When I teach C.L.A.S.S., on the first morning I review four major points: Problem, Purpose, Plan, and Personality. These are clearly written in the workbook and each time I move on to a new one I review the previous ones. The fifth "P" is Practice and when I get to this I mention it but I don't make a point of this "P" being the conclusion of the list. The next morning I have the audience recite back the outline showing what they learned. They all recall the first four clearly, but when asked for the fifth, no one remembers what it was. Even though it was printed in the same type as the others and I mentioned it once, it does not stay in their minds.

If you want anything remembered state it, explain it, and repeat it. Start each meeting with the yearly purpose and the goal for that meeting. "This year we wish to double our membership and our aim today is to plan the membership tea."

Before you start your term in office find a copy of the bylaws and read them. This step alone will make you ABOVE AVERAGE as no one else even knows you have any—and possibly you don't!

You may find some original purposes that have long been ignored or some ideas that will make your yearly plan more vital.

When I was elected president of the Women's Club of San Bernardino I read the bylaws and found one of our neglected goals was to foster spiritual values in our members. On this principle I had the grounds to start a Bible study in our clubhouse and initiate a prayer breakfast. For our efforts, we won a special state award for spiritual values and ethics and were instrumental in organizing district, state, and ultimately, national prayer breakfasts.

Know all you can about the background and bylaws of your organization, adopt a realistic goal for the year, and repeat your purpose or slogan often enough to make them remember it and want to achieve it.

*Preparation:*The big secret in confident leadership is in being prepared. There is no way you can be consistent in conducting your meetings if you run in at the last minute and try to pull the thing together. We had a pastor once who often came to the Wednesday night Bible study with no idea of what he was going to do. When he was prepared he would walk in briskly, go immediately to the pulpit and present an exciting program. On those nights when he would come in casually and shake hands with every person in an aisle seat, I knew he wasn't ready and prayed the Holy Sprit would reveal a three-point outline to him as he wandered through the church.

Preparation is essential for your own self-confidence and for the comfort of the people. When you are agitated, they get nervous.

How to prepare for a meeting—Take out a pad of paper and for your own benefit, write the purpose of the club and the goal for the day across the top of your page. If you don't know what your goal is, it's more difficult to achieve it. This page will become your practice agenda. Start by listing all the regular items of business.

Call to order—"Will the October 15th meeting of the Women's Club of San Bernardino please come to order."

Thought-for-the-day or opening prayer—To make your job easier it is well to assign a responsible person who will give this opening thought. If the designated person forgets to come, it is the one who made the assignment who must fill in. Delegate every job possible so that your mind is free to conduct the meeting and have it all make sense.

Pledge of Allegiance—If your group is not this formal, list whatever routine items must be handled in the beginning.

Secretary's report—The best way to keep this report clear and concise and not a review of the secretary's recent vacation to Hawaii is to make it a policy right from the beginning that she write her report within twenty-four hours of the meeting and get a copy in your hands within three days. This practice increases the chances for accuracy and gives you the time to correct errors and cross out trivia. After you have updated her report, return it with a note of praise for how few things you had to add or delete. This plaudit will make her want to do better next time and keep her from resenting your corrections.

At the end of her report ask: "Are there any errors or ommissions?" If there are not say, "The report is approved as read." If there are, accept them, and then say, "The report is approved as corrected." If you also have a corresponding secretary, have her read any notes or letters at this point.

Treasurer's report—Since most women go to sleep at the mention of a budget, you should see that this report is as brief as possible. I always made sure I knew what the figures were about and I gave a review of what the treasurer had said for clarity. Sometimes the report is just read for information, but other groups want a chance to discuss the finances. Conclude with, "The treasurer's report is approved as read" or "The treasurer's report is approved as corrected."

Some organizations print up the treasurer's report, pass it out to all and don't read it in the meeting.

Old business—Whatever is pending from the last meeting should be dealt with first, so list these items. The best way to know you won't forget something is to read over your collection of minutes from the last few meetings. I would always review the minutes from the previous year to spot some matter that should be brought up every October or every January.

After each item is announced and discussed, the presiding officer is to ask for a motion on the subject. It is best if *you* state a possible motion that is clear and will allow for either a yes or no response. It is never the chairman's prerogative to give per-

Names	AGENDA
	Date_____
	Purpose:
	Call to order
_____	**Thought or prayer**
_____	**Pledge of Allegiance**
_____	**Secretary's report**
_____	**Corresponding secretary's report**
_____	**Treasurer's report**
	Old business
_____	_____
_____	_____
	New business
_____	_____
_____	_____
	Committee reports
_____	_____
_____	_____
	Miscellaneous items
_____	_____
_____	_____
	Adjournment
_____	**Program Introduction**
_____	**Closing remarks and/or prayer**

This sample agenda is to give you an idea of how to prepare for a meeting that will be done "decently and in order." Some of you will strip this down to meet the simplicity of your small committee and a few of you may want to expand it. If you wish to have a deeper understanding of parliamentary procedure, study *Robert's Rules of Order*, the Bible of leadership.

sonal opinions which will sway the group. When a motion is made, ask for a second to that motion. Then repeat the motion as stated, say it has been made and seconded, and instruct, "All those in favor, please say aye. All opposed, please say no." There is no reason to take a count unless the vote is in question. Then say, "The ayes have it and we have just voted to...."

New business—The procedure will be the same as old business except that many of these items may be suggested by other members. My policy was to have the suggestion or motion in writing ahead of the meeting or it would not be discussed. Members actually like the meetings better because they are brief and purposeful. Your attendance will rise or fall according to the interest or the boredom of your meetings.

Committee reports—In order to keep chairmen working, you must allow them to report their progress and commend them for whatever step forward they may have made. As with new business, I always asked the chairmen to let me know before the meeting if they intended to give a report so that I could place them on the agenda.

Miscellaneous items—Your group may have some specialized items or announcements that must be made at this point. Discourage personal pet projects that can drag the meeting down.

At this point thank everyone who has done anything remotely significant. Since most women thrive on praise and plaudits, please give them. Consistent compliments and credit will place you way ABOVE AVERAGE.

Adjournment—Ask for any last minute items of business and then say, "I declare the meeting of the (name of organization) to be adjourned."

Program—If there is to be a program, adjourn the formal meeting and then call upon the program chairman to introduce the speaker. Your job should be over unless a wrap-up or benediction is needed at the end.

• • •

Now that you have written the practice agenda and have filled in all the business reports, set the paper aside for a few days. As ideas or phone calls come in, add to the page. The day before the meeting, reread, correct, and type the final agenda. When I had my finished copy in hand, I would then underline the major items in colors so that I could pick them out at a glance. In the margin I would add the name of the person who was doing the prayer, the secretary, the report chairman, et cetera, in big print next to their item. I never assumed I would remember my best friend's name when up front so I listed everyone in color. I could see the names easily and therefore never stumbled or wondered who this was approaching.

When you know your agenda is complete, run off some copies for the secretary, the vice-president, and the parliamentarian or any other people who need to have an itemized list of the day's proceedings. On the first meeting when you walk in with a neat agenda in triplicate, the word will spread quickly that they have a president who is ABOVE AVERAGE.

In your preparation to lead your group, it is essential that you have some place in your home that is just for this club's materials. If you don't have a desk, try for a drawer, briefcase, or at least a box. The minute anything comes in for this organization, put it in the proper place. If you let papers drift around the house waiting for a day to sort them out, you may never see them again. I had one secretary in a women's club who left her minutes on the kitchen counter. When she went to find them, they were gone and she arrived without a report. At the next meeting she told us her son had picked them up by mistake, had stapled them into the middle of his college term paper, and they had received a B + .

Even if you have a correspondence secretary, you should go through the mail. She may not know what you consider important or how you want a note answered. At a time-management seminar I learned: Handle each piece of mail only once. As you read the letter for the first time, underline what needs attention and write the name of who should take action on this item. Before each meeting hand out the mail to those who should follow through and hope for the best.

Presentation: On the day when you are to preside (introduce the speaker or give an announcement), arrive early with your wisdom and wits about you. Pass out your agendas to those who need a copy and open the meeting on time. Remember, you set the tone on clothing, manners, and punctuality. If there is a microphone, use it since there are frequently ladies who are hard of hearing.

Many women are terrified of anything mechanical and pull back while expressing, "I have a loud voice. I don't need a mike." I have learned that women who are boistrous and even garrulous off stage often times act just the opposite when giving the flea market report. I ignore their "loud voice" comments and with a firm hand on the shoulder ease them into the mike. To give others courage to speak up, you must be confident in using the equipment yourself even if you must come an hour early to practice.

In the thirty years I have been involved with all types of club, church and organizational work, I have found that when the presiding officer leads with loving authority, the group will follow with respect. But if she is insecure, nervous, and confused they will swoop in upon her as vultures. If you know the purpose of your position, have a clear goal for the year, have done your homework, arrive early and prepared, you will preside with confidence.

It Takes So Little To Be ABOVE AVERAGE.

3

It Takes So Little To Entertain Above Average

23

Be a Lover of Hospitality

Be a lover of hospitality, a lover of good men, sober, just, holy, temperate.

Titus 1:8

I have always been a "lover of hospitality." I've had parties for any possible reason and celebrated every holiday known to man. Over the years I've collected decorations and centerpieces for every season and have known where they were for display at the right time. As my children grew up, they became lovers of hospitality also. We have had extra people living with us off and on for thirty years and entertaining strangers has been a way of life.

After our family all dedicated their lives to the Lord, He moved us from our comfortable social position in Connecticut, where our house was used for the "opening teas" of everything, to "Bungalow One" in California. Looking back on it, the Lord really had a sense of humor to take a person who had spent her life working up to the big home and the country club, then plunk her into a dilapidated, abandoned bungalow. Hadn't He promised me an abundant, not abandoned, life? Why was I sentenced to hard labor in a shell of a motel? When we had been asked to go on staff with Campus Crusade for Christ I somehow pictured Fred and me on a spiritual cloud floating through life with the greats of the faith while a choir sang majestically in the background. How quickly I fell off the cloud when I found I was to live in "Bungalow One"—five motel rooms, each with a door opening out onto a patio. There wasn't even a kitchen so I had to cook for my family on a hot plate on a porch. How could anyone be a lover of hospitality in such a setting?

Oh what a lesson the Lord had in mind for me! He had to teach me that it wasn't the surroundings but the spirit that made for genuine hospitality. As a family, we crowded into those five little rooms and, to put us to a further test, the Lord sent "strangers" to live with us. We had four girls layered in one room and when my mother came to visit, we added a third bunkbed on the top of one set where Marita lay each night with her head inches from the ceiling. Young Fred and nephew Dwayne were in bunks in the next room and Fred and I had a motel room at the far end.

We made the porch into a kitchen and we ate a few feet from the sink. The table filled all the available space and whoever sat in the back couldn't get out short of a fire. There was no place to shelve all my assorted sets of dishes and my centerpieces were retired in storage to "Bungalow Two." I had come full circle. After the great climb to success I was back in "three rooms behind the store."

Could I ever entertain in "Bungalow One"? With eight around a crowded table every night, could we add even one more? Psalm 101:6 says, "I will make the godly of the land my heroes and invite them to my home" (TLB). Surely the godly of the land passed through Arrowhead Springs and I found what they wanted most was a friendly, home-cooked meal. Since I spend so much of my time traveling alone and in motels eating by myself, I can understand how they enjoyed our home life. I can see why the spirit of togetherness was more important than the space.

I became the "Martha of the Hill," cooking and serving the godly of the Lord. Dr. Henry Brandt sat at our table many nights and I learned from him the skills of counseling. So much of what I do automatically today came from the hours of advice I received from Dr. Brandt. Toni Florio and his family fellowshipped with us and he shared with me his counseling experiences. Howard Blandau helped Lauren adjust to this unexpected move in her early teen years and black evangelist Ernie Wilson held my little 5-year-old Fred in his arms on each visit. Eleanor Whitney taught me much about Christian speaking and Barbara Fain schooled me as a Bible study teacher. Ian Thomas enthralled us all with his English accent and Hal Lindsey introduced us to prophecy. Christian speakers and leaders from all over the world crowded into "Bungalow One" and filled our family reservoirs with rich experiences.

Could I ever entertain in "Bungalow One"? Oh, yes. I could and did. Hospitality doesn't depend on size, but on spirit. In fact the dictionary says hospitality is "the spirit of being hospitable," which is "behaving in a kind and generous manner toward guests, fond of entertaining. (Latin Hospes = guest, Hospitore = to entertain)[1]

While I was living in "Bungalow One," I was asked to give the Campus Crusade staff instructions on "courtesy and manners" and also to teach a Christian living course at a local church. During my time of preparation for these two classes, I interviewed over two hundred people on their experiences and attitudes on entertaining. I started with the assumption that everyone did entertain, devising a chart for people to check off how often, how many people, and for what kind of an occasion. Much to my surprise I found few had anybody in for any reason. These results shifted my emphasis from *how* to entertain to *why*.

Why should Christians entertain? The Bible tells us to use hospitality one to another without grudging (1 Peter 4:9). Peter tells us to open up our homes without complaining. How often I hear a woman bemoaning the fact that she has to have some people over. How much fun will these people have? How do I feel when a lady tells me she can't come to my seminar because she's been assigned to cook my dinner and it will take her all day. As she sighs, I wonder if I'm worth eight hours of preparation. Wouldn't it be better if she came to the sessions? We would then have a mutual subject for conversation while letting the "Colonel" do the cooking.

> *Be not forgetful to entertain strangers for thereby some have entertained angels unawares.*
>
> *Hebrews 13:2*

In our two years in "Bungalow One" and in the following years, we have entertained many strangers who turned out to be angels. I remember one time bringing home a visiting missionary nurse who was on leave from Zaire. None of us knew much about Zaire and, up until then, had not cared to. One family policy we have adopted is to always ask the guest to explain what it is he or she does. Frequently these people are shy and will not push into the conversation of a verbose family. Fred encourages them to share and we then can get the benefits we might have missed.

Young Fred, ten years old at the time, brought out his globe so the nurse could show him where Zaire was. She held him spellbound as she explained a culture to him he'd never known existed. That night when she showed slides at church he was in the front row.

What a unanimous benefit it can be to entertain strangers, but remember to encourage them into sharing or you will miss the blessing.

> *Distributing to the necessity of the saints; given to hospitality.*
>
> Romans 12:13

The Bible says we should open our homes to strangers. Yes, get into the habit of entertaining even overnight. It's much easier to get out of the habit than it is to get into it. Feeding groups at a moment's notice is not easy but as you get in the habit, it can be fun. I always made sure to have staples on hand for certain basic dishes and when Fred let me know at five o'clock that a few friends were in town, I was able to put together an adequate meal—remembering that no one expects a gourmet treat, they just enjoy a simple meal at home.

As I was raising my children they always got excited about having company "overnight," whether it was their friends or strangers. They all knew they could bring home anyone who needed a place to stay and we have "thereby" entertained many "angels unawares."

In I Timothy 3:2 we learn that a Christian leader was to be "given to hospitality" and in chapter five, verse ten that a godly woman must have "lodged strangers and washed the saint's feet."

Aren't you glad we now have showers?
Why should Christians entertain? Because the Bible tells us so.

It Takes So Little To Be ABOVE AVERAGE.

24

Entertain Strangers and Saints

If we know we should be lovers of hospitality *why don't we entertain more often*? The following are actual excuses I've been given. Have you ever used one of these?

My house is too small. How big was "Bungalow One"? When one lady told me she had never had me over because her house was too small, I asked, "How big do you think I am? I only need one average size chair." She thought it over for a minute and replied, "I guess I've been using that as an excuse for years. I figured if you didn't have a big house you didn't have to have company."

My house isn't decorated yet. I have one friend who told me for ten years she'd have me over when she got the house done. Once I arrived unexpectedly to deliver something to her and she kept me out on the front step because the house wasn't ready. I really expected someday that the great unveiling would come, but she moved away before that happened.

I don't have good china. Who cares? I happen to love all kinds of beautiful china, but if you'll feed me, I sure won't care if the dishes even match. If this problem is not just an excuse, watch for bargains.

I'm not a good cook. Now there's a *real* excuse, or is it? One Sunday in the Calendar section of the *Los Angeles Times* I counted forty different cooking classes in the area. Recipes abound in every women's magazine and there is the *Too Busy To Cook* cookbook that guarantees a gourmet meal in thirty minutes. One evening I was served an excellent creamed chicken on flaky pastry shells and when I complimented the hostess, she said, "I'm really not a good cook but I don't let that keep me from entertaining. I bought a few pouches of Stouffer's Creamed Chicken and heated up the frozen shells. Most people seem to like it."

I'm too disorganized. If you don't know how to organize your household, read a book like *More Hours in My Day* by Emilie Barnes. If you don't have time to read it today but you have to entertain tomorrow, I'll give you a plan in a few pages.

My mother never entertained. Having been brought up eating in the grocery store with customers watching, I was surely never steeped in the social graces. In college I took out books on etiquette and watched the housemother serve. I'm still reading and learning from others.

I don't have enough money. If this is a valid excuse, you might consider having people over for coffee after church or hosting an occasional potluck supper. People don't mind bringing something to eat if you'll do the set-up and clean-up.

I don't know who to ask. I find people to ask on every corner, but then I find people on every corner. Fred and I have always made it a custom to look around for new faces in church and invite them home for Sunday brunch. We have met new friends this way and many have said they kept coming to the church because we were friendly. When I was president of the women's club I got a list of all the little ladies who were going to be alone for Christmas. I passed around a sign-up sheet for those members who would like to have them yet no one put her name on the list. When I asked around, the answer was, "Christmas is a personal holiday and we don't want any outsiders around."

We don't like the same people. This is often just an excuse but sometimes it is a problem. The wife has all Christian friends and the husband's friends "might swear." One man told me, "All her friends are so d——— saintly that it makes me sick!" It is important that we don't turn each dinner party into a tent meeting turning off the nonbelievers. Have your Bible studies in the daytime and your evangelistic girl friends for lunch and aim for dinner guests with whom your husband can feel comfortable.

Fred and I have been victims of evenings when at dessert the hostess would say, "Now you two give your testimony," hoping we would save her husband over apple pie. We went to a party one night where the lady had promised her husband she wouldn't do anything religious. However, she had invited a young man to give an evangelistic talk and end with an invitation prayer. As the surprise guest spoke, her husband shifted in his seat and was obviously upset at this sneaky program. To make him think it wasn't really religious she jumped in right after the "Amen" and said "Let's all sing a chorus or two of 'There's a Shanty in Old Shanty Town.' " Somewhat aghast we all weakly sang about the shanties as her husband disappeared from view. Not all saints and sinners are socially compatible but it is possible to win the world with a loving spirit without ever quoting a verse.

People don't come on time. Isn't that the truth! But don't expect them to come on time. If I want to serve dinner at 7:00 P.M. I have them come at 6:30 and have some snacks and punch available. I make sure I don't have many last-minute things to do and I never put the rolls in until the roll's been called.

People don't leave on time. They must be having a good time! If this is a genuine problem, state on the invitation 7:00-9:00 P.M. or say on the phone, "We have to be up early the next day so we'll be finishing up about nine." We once had some people who just wouldn't leave so Fred finally stood up and said, "I hope you'll excuse me but I must get to bed." This is not the most gracious thing to do, but in desperation it will work.

People don't ask us back. Join the club! In my social days I used to keep a record of what people had us so I could keep even. Once a good friend told me, "I'm not inviting you over for Sunday night because when I checked I didn't owe you a dinner." As I began to study Christian hospitality I found in Luke 14:12-14, "...'When you put on a dinner,' he said, 'don't invite friends, brothers, relatives, and rich neighbors! For they will return the invitation. Instead, invite the poor, the crippled, the lame, and the blind. Then at the resurrection of the godly, God will reward you for inviting those who can't repay you' " (TLB). From these verses I learned that I was to be a lover of hospitality without ever expecting anything in return. While in "Bungalow One" almost all the people I entertained were those passing through town. I knew they would never have me back, but how much I gained from the fellowship of the saints.

If these are only excuses then *what are the underlying reasons of why we don't entertain.*

>   ***Worry***—"I'm just sick for days before I have anyone over."
>   ***Fear of Failure***—"What if it doesn't turn out right?"
>   ***Pride***—"If I can't do it perfectly, I'm not going to do it at all."
>   ***Bitterness***—"No one ever has us over and I'll just show
>   them."
>   ***Selfishness***—"We're all so busy that when we have a spare
>   minute we just want to be alone."
>   ***Laziness***—"It's so much easier to stop by McDonald's."

As we agree that the Bible instructs us to entertain and we see the excuses or reasons why we don't, we can conclude that in the field of Christian hospitality—

It Takes So Little To Be ABOVE AVERAGE.

25

Prepare a Table

The virtuous woman got up before dawn to prepare breakfast and she bought food imported from afar. She also spent time each morning giving her servant girls instructions and right there most of us lose contact with her. If we entertain, we have to do all the work and it seems overwhelming.

How can we make entertaining fun? First decide what type of entertaining you want to do. If you're inexperienced or unsure of yourself, don't start with an elegant dinner party for twelve. What are different possiblities?

Instead of the **sit-down dinner** where you may feel like a glorified waitress, you could try a **buffet supper** where the food is prepared, laid out on a buffet table, and guests serve themselves. They can sit at one table, several small tables, or on any available chair or couch.

The **potluck**, or covered dish supper, can be set up the same as the buffet but the guests bring at least part of the food. For several years, when we lived in a large home, Fred and I had a potluck once a month on Saturday for any friends, plus their friends, who wanted to come. We did not assign specific items and it usually came out about right. We set up tables all over the house and I made matching tablecloths and napkins from sheets. I provided the house, prepared the tables, made coffee and tea, and cleaned up afterwards. Each time we had some kind of entertainment or program. If a singing group was in town or a traveling speaker, we'd invite them to share. One February we prepared all kinds of material for making valentines and gave prizes for the most creative. We averaged about fifty people and sometimes had up to ninety. It took ABOVE AVERAGE effort, but many remember the evenings of fun and fellowship.

Barbecues make entertaining simple especially if your husband likes to cook. When weather permits, set up a picnic table, have hamburgers and rolls, an assortment of relishes, and perhaps a salad. Men seem to be most relaxed when standing over the flames of a charcoal burner.

I like to have company for **brunch** because Fred makes crepes. After church I set the table while he prepares the batter and makes coffee and by the time the guests arrive we're ready to go. All we need on the table is butter and syrup although often we add fruit and sour cream. People love to watch Fred cook and he keeps at it as long as anyone will eat. The fellowship after church is relaxed and unpressured and no one expects a big meal.

Theme parties, birthdays or showers. Because we are a creative family, we love to come up with different kinds of parties that have a theme. We've celebrated Ground Hog Day and even the appointment of a new pope! For our twenty-fifth anniversary Marita and Lauren gave us a surprise party. We had just moved from our big house to a condominium with strawberry-covered wallpaper in the kitchen. The girls sent invitations on strawberry note cards and everyone was instructed to bring a strawberry gift wrapped in strawberry paper. For refreshments they served bowls of huge strawberries and had strawberry punch.

For Fred's fiftieth birthday we had a 1950s party and everyone was to wear what they would have been wearing in the '50s. I wore my honeymoon going-away suit of bright red poodle cloth and Marita was adorable in baby clothes with a ruffled bonnet. We had '50s music and relived our youth.

When Marita's book, *Shades of Beauty,* was published in July 1982, we wanted to give her a "success" party. Lauren tied rainbow ribbons to each rosebush that lined the entry and put a huge rainbow over the front door. She sent rainbow card invitations, had rainbow napkins, and a large rainbow arched across the cake. Lauren lined pictures of Marita in her various life stages across the wall and everyone shared what part they had played in Marita's climb to success.

With a little thought and planning any party can be ABOVE AVERAGE.

Coffees and teas are about the simplest type of entertaining you can do and often the most fun for all because you are relaxed. In these hurried days where few entertain formally, an invitation for coffee is welcomed. If you have some cookies or cheese and crackers, bring those out, but a sociable hour around a cup of coffee can be a blessed time of sharing.

Let's assume you've chosen to have a simple dinner party and you want it to go smoothy. What are some guidelines you can follow?

PLAN

1. Make out a simple menu using dishes you know how to prepare. Don't choose a crucial moment to try your first souffle.
2. Make a list of every ingredient you need to buy and check those you think you have. Finding out at the last minute that your children have eaten a vital ingredient can ruin your evening.
3. Make a list of everything that has to be done. As your children grow up you can assign them duties. I always made up a list of the items to be served, what platter or dish they were to go on and who was responsible for putting it on the table. For example:

    Meat and potatoes—Wooden Trencher—Florence
    Tossed Salad—Black bowl with silver base—Lauren
    Bread (heated)—Straw basket—Marita
    Butter—Crystal butter dish—Fred, Jr.
    Water (fill glasses)—Silver pitcher—Fred, Sr.

    We all had our duties and handled them at the right time.
4. Check off the list as you go along. This prevents you from forgetting the rolls until they're burned black or finishing the whole meal with the relish tray still in the refrigerator.

PREPARE

1. Do the marketing a day ahead. On times when I haven't followed my own advice, I've been running from store to store at the last minute to find lady fingers for the chocolate mousse I haven't made yet that has to set three hours.

2. Prepare everything as early as possible. Never assume you'll have a lot of time in the afternoon. Each one of us could write pages about emergencies that have ruined the best laid plans.
3. Set the table early in the day. I've often done it the night before. Seeing that table set is a tranquilizer for you as you race around and it's soothing to the guests also when they see you are indeed prepared.
4. Try to clean up the kitchen before the guests arrive. There is nothing more unnerving to the guests than to drift into your kitchen and find open cans sitting around, cooking dishes piled high in the sink and batter dribbling into the open silver drawer. Conversely, I've been complimented by guests who have commented, "I would never know you'd cooked a meal here."
5. Allow plenty of time to dress. I still have trouble realizing how long it takes to get dressed even though I've been late many times. I now give myself twice what I think it will take and I come out about even.

PRESENT

1. Present yourself attractively at the door. I've been met at people's doors by all kinds of visions: rollers in the hair, nightgowns, bathing suits. What's worse is when no one comes or some little unknown child opens the door. One evening Fred and I stood in a foyer trying to converse with a four-year-old and hoping we were in the right house.
2. Greet your guests warmly. Tell them how glad you are they could come. Don't let them sense tension or fear to make them ill at ease. If you have to go right back to the kitchen either seat them with your husband or a child or ask if they'd like to join you while you finish up the preparation. The tone of their first few minutes in your home gives them a mind-set for the evening.
3. Be natural, yet not trying to impress. There is nothing that unnerves a guest so quickly as your trying to impress them with your great works. I've been in situations where the dear lady chronicled her whole week of preparing this dinner until I felt guilty I'd come. Be yourself. No one likes a phony, so relax. Even if something fails, it won't ruin your life or theirs.

4. Don't keep apologizing. "I got started so late today, I'll never get this on the table"; "I bet this is too sweet for you"; "This is a new recipe and I'm scared to death that it won't be right"; "I'm such a bad cook I don't know why I invited you." I've had all these said to me, some by the same lady in the same night. I'd like the hostess to do her best and not hover over me in a sea of worry. Constant apologies make everyone nervous.

5. Don't point out your mistakes because we might not even notice and knowing might ruin the meal. "I ran out of sugar so I used blackstrap molasses"; "After I mixed this all up I said to myself, 'This looks just like dog food' "; "This cake wasn't supposed to be an upside down cake but it sure is now. I dropped it on the floor but I brushed it off and I vacuumed yesterday anyway"; "I burned the carrots so pretend they're carmelized." None of these errors, pointed out to guests, adds to one's appetite. As Julia Child says, "What they don't know won't hurt them." If you don't point out your mistakes, few people will ever notice them.

PARTICIPATE

1. Don't spend all your time in the kitchen. Guests would much rather have a simple meal with you at the table than something so complex you rarely show up. Fred and I had dinner one time where the hostess didn't even set herself a place. She explained, "I really want my guests to have a good time so I do all I can to make them happy." She meant well but we all felt uncomfortable as she ferried courses in and out of the kitchen by herself. When guests come to your home they want to visit so plan something that you can handle easily. How can we relax when you're so overworked?

2. Ask people to help you. It is not a sign of weakness to ask someone to assist you. I plan ahead what small jobs others can do and find they feel better doing something than sitting alone in the living room. Guests can take snacks or hor d'oeuvres to each other, they can man the punchbowl or pass out napkins. They can take a head count on coffee or tea and serve the dessert while you rinse the dishes. Always remember your aim is to treat the guests to a relaxing evening not impress them with how hard you've worked just for them.

3. Have your husband participate. If your husband is willing, include him in your plans. Have him answer the door and take coats, get a beverage for the guests, keep them happy in the living room. Don't let him think this is your thing and he's too inept to help. I can always tell how a man is treated at home by how he reacts when I ask him to help me. If I ask a man to carry the punchbowl to the patio and he says, "Me? You want me to carry this glass bowl? You trust me?" I know he feels like a dummy at home. For some reason he's not a contributing part of the family. Make your husband feel an important part of the festivities.

4. Have something for children to do. If you are still in the era when little ones arrive, it is well to plan what to do with them ahead of time. I often seated them at a separate table and had little favors or gifts to keep them happy. I usually fed them first so they could play in another room while we ate. Once when we had a big holiday party and I wanted our dinner to be special with no distractions, I hired a young girl across the street to come for two hours. Lauren made up sandwiches, chips and cupcakes and put a little lunch for each child in separate bags. Just before the adults sat down to eat we summoned the children and Lauren told them how much fun they were going to have on their picnic. They weren't to open their bags until they got to the picnic table we had set up in a vacant lot nearby. The sitter led them off so excited and all of us had a pleasant meal.

5. Have a "Plan B" in mind if conversation fails. There are times when all the guests are brilliant and you wouldn't interrupt the flow for anything, but there are those evenings when nothing seems to click. What do you do? Fred and I have several "Plan Bs." We have had times when a quiet group came alive with some structured conversation. "Since many of you don't know each other let's go around the table and introduce ourselves. Tell where you grew up, what schools you went to, what interests you have that are unusual and what you'd do if you had all next week off with no responsiblity." Always start with yourself since what you say will set the tone. If you share for five minutes they will too. If you give it all in one sentence that's all they will do.

One Mother's Day we had all the guests tell what they

remembered about their mothers in their childhood. We had tender and touching stories exchanged. One Christmas we had each person tell what had been the most significant event in their past year. On Valentine's Day we asked about our childhood sweethearts and what became of them. Several times we've asked what goals people have in their personal growth and how can they achieve them. Other guests begin to give suggestions. It's amazing how people will respond when you first lead with a question of interest and then give the first example yourself.

Time is so valuable we cannot afford to waste it on purposeless chatter. In our family we now have five adult men: Father Fred; Fred; Lauren's husband, Randy; Marita's husband, Chuck; and Brenda's husband, Ken. (Brenda lived with us for many years and is like part of the family.) Father Fred realized how little time he spent with the boys, so he scheduled a once-a-month men's night. He takes them all out to a restaurant for dinner and leads them in some structured conversation. As they share their feelings about their childhoods, their careers, and their goals, they really get to know each other. My husband looks forward to hosting times of true fellowship and he senses a new love and understanding among the family men.

So many people have something fascinating to say but they don't think anyone cares to hear it. You be the one to coordinate the conversation, keeping it as even as possible so one person doesn't monopolize the night.

If you are a lover of hospitality desiring to entertain strangers and saints and willing to prepare a table for others, you will delight the Lord and your guests.

It Takes So Little To Be ABOVE AVERAGE.

F

It Takes So Little To Care Above Average

26

Relieve the Afflicted

As I organized my topics for this book, I asked myself what kind of women would want to learn to become ABOVE AVERAGE. I saw the need for a time of self-evaluation for myself before stepping out to lead others. From teaching C.L.A.S.S., I knew women became excited when they began to think more creatively. I had also learned of the desire for leadership training among Christian women. From my experience in many business meetings, I knew the average chairman was below average. I had observed how few Christians were really "lovers of hospitality" and what an effort it seemed to be to "entertain the saints." I was confident that all of these areas needed to be dealt with in a clear and encouraging manner and I set out to write with excitement. Way in the back of my mind was the seed of a thought. How does the average Christian treat the person with problems? How do we love the unlovable, the undesirable, the unpopular? What do we do with the ugly and the odd? How do we handle death, divorce, and despair?

Although I did not plan to cover these questions, these thoughts did not go away. One day I presented this problem to the Lord and said, "If You want me to deal with these difficult dilemmas, show me." The next day I boarded a plane and sat in my customary bulkhead window seat. The aisle seat was taken and the middle seat empty. At the last minute a handsome young man, obviously distressed, plunked down next to me and said, "I'll never fly this airline again!" Since the Lord consistently sends me fascinating "plane partners," I inquired about his problem. After relating his annoyance, he calmed down and we began to discuss our lives and careers. I told him I was writing a book on how to be ABOVE AVERAGE. He asked how I chose writing as a career and I then gave him my testimony. When I got to the part about my two brain-damaged sons, I saw his expression change.

"I have a little girl with Apert's Syndrome," he whispered. "Perhaps you'll understand what we've been through." He told me how little Jennifer had been born with cranioserosis, a fusion of the sutures in the skull, and syndactyly, a fusion of the fingers.

"When I first saw her I prayed she'd die. They told us she'd need surgery if she lived and she did."

He told me how he checked his insurance and found it didn't cover birth defects or any surgery relating to them. He went to the March of Dimes but they could only give $300.00 if he agreed to accept no other charity. He needed $20,000. Handicapped Children's Services was going to help but the state funds were cut off the week before the surgery. He called the governor's office but they wouldn't talk to him; the lieutenant governor said it was out of his jurisdiction. A senator promised to call back but later said he had no funds. The case worker agreed they had tried everything and it was impossible to get money for the surgery. In desperation he called the state legislature and finally someone referred him to the state emergency funds. A sympathetic ear heard his case and agreed to pay for the operation.

In two and one half years baby Jennifer has had nine surgeries, still needs five or six more, and she still looks extremley abnormal. By the time this dear young man had poured out his problems we were both in tears. I consoled him and he cried, "You're the first one who's understood."

I told him I had been debating about a chapter on how to treat people with unusual problems and that I'd prayed that the Lord would direct me. I asked if he'd share how people had reacted and he said, "The most difficult thing is friends who are not supportive. Some wouldn't come to our house any more for fear it would be contagious." He went on to give examples of what unthinking people said as I continued to take notes.

Strangers ask, "What's wrong with her hands?" A man in a store said, "Good Lord, that child is deformed." One mother pointed out to her children, "Look at that ugly baby!" and another called her little ones over and exclaimed, "This baby looks just like E.T.!"

I shared with him how I got a call from a friend when my first little boy was very ill asking if I knew that Lauren arrived at school each day crying. When I asked her, she admitted she was in tears because the children on the bus teased her calling out, "Your brother's a moron." "Why didn't you tell me?" "I knew you had so much on your mind, I didn't want to upset you any more."

The young man and I agreed it is the parent who points out these problems to the children. I asked if I could share his story with others and he replied, "If it will help one person to be more sensitive to the abnormal child, it will be worth it. Please tell them, if you can't say something nice, say nothing."

I changed planes in Dallas, boarding the next one and sitting in the same seat location. A lady sat next to me with her eight-year-old son by the aisle. She turned to me and said, "I'm not very happy with this airline. They didn't have three seats together and my husband had to sit in the back." This sounded like an echo of the first man's words. By then her boy was standing on the seat looking around. As she pulled him down she asked if I'd ever had a "hyperactive boy" like this one. I told her briefly of my two sons and she said soberly, "You too?"

She then gave me a long history of her 18-year-old retarded and crippled daughter, Ruth, and of the relatives who kept asking her, "What did you do to cause this?" She said children seemed to accept Ruth better than adults and one child frequently came to the door and asked, "Can I play with your little crippled girl?"

As we shared some of the heartache of a parent with abnormal children, we both agreed: People don't mean to be cruel, they just don't know what to say.

From these two very similar experiences the day after I prayed for direction, I decided I *must* write on how to handle people with traumas. I mentioned the subject at the next C.L.A.S.S. and women came up with case histories. It seemed everywhere I went I found new examples. As I sorted through them I realized that whatever the problem, people did the same things correctly or reacted the same way incorrectly. General principles of positive and negative behavior appeared and I will share some helpful suggestions with you.

In searching for verses and a title for this chapter I found 1 Timothy 5:10, "Relieve the afflicted." To make sure I understood the meaning clearly I looked in the dictionary. Relieve means "to free from pain or embarrassment." The afflicted are "those depressed with continued suffering, misfortune or calamity." If you and I are to *relieve* the afflicted we must try to ease their pain and not embarrass them. So many of the cases I was told about had relatives or friends who added guilt to their pain and often hurt or ridiculed them in front of others. If you and I are to relieve the *afflicted*, we must help anyone we know who is distressed or depressed and who is suffering the loss of a loved one, the misfortune of a divorce or the calamity of cancer. The list of those with continued suffering is endless. If you and I want to be ABOVE AVERAGE in relieving the afflicted what should we do?

Not everyone has the gift of mercy or helps but we can all learn to be sensitive and to care. Let's start with some things *not* to do.

DON'TS

Don't preach or judge: Somehow the Christian world feels called upon to preach to the afflicted. One lady sent me a note saying: "I got tons of advice, well-meant, and strongly delivered, full of certainty, and all conflicting." One woman I know was married to a Baptist preacher. He went through a midlife crisis and ran off with a young parishioner. The wife had done everything she could to pull things back together when another pastor told her, "You can be forgiven for the sin of divorce just as you could for murder or stealing." God may lump them all together but when you are hurting, to be told you're the same as a murderer or thief surely does not relieve the pain.

Don't say, "If you were really a Christian...": When my second son was still alive, I'd occasionally have a dear little lady come up to me after I spoke and say, "If you were really a Christian you'd have your son home with you where he belongs." Since many of us in crises have only the Lord Jesus to depend on, it is devastating to have someone question your Christian commitment.

Don't say, "That's not how you're supposed to feel": There's no standard rule on feelings and in crisis times they may change minute by minute. "You should be happy; he's gone to heaven" does not cheer the bereaved. Whether the victim is weeping or smiling for the moment, being told, "That's not how you're supposed to feel," only makes things worse.

Don't label others as "Tools of the devil": This cliche is used frequently to excuse why things go wrong. "That counselor who told you that was surely a tool of the devil." How do you know? How can it help to pin a label on? How will the designated person feel when he learns what you've called him?

Don't tell horror stories: I remember when my mother was in bed with phlebitis and a friend came in to cheer her up. She told her of a lady who had the exact symptoms and was dead within the hour. Edith Lanstrom wrote me about coping with a mastectomy. "Do not let other persons invade your environment with negativity. Politely but firmly cut off cancer horror stories. You are already aware of them and don't need to be reminded."

Don't tell of those who had miracles: Equally disturbing are stories of those who were so pure that God healed them, leaving the recipient of the anecdote wondering what's wrong with her. It's good to hold out hope, but be sure not to add the feeling of failure or sin to the person who is already depressed or dying.

Don't write them off: How many times I've been told of permanent rifts in families because one said, "If you do this, I'll write you off"; or to a teenager, "If you ever get pregnant don't bother to come home"—and she disappears; "If you marry him I never want to see you again"; "If you don't go to my doctor, I'll wash my hands of your whole problem." Statements like these show we're more interested in having our way than in loving the needy.

When her husband walked out on her, one lady said, her mother repeatedly reminded her of two things: "1) There would be *no way* I could survive financially; 2) I had better not expect any help from her." She goes on to say:

> I expect this may be a secret worry in many families. The sweet thing is that her letter this week did contain a small amount of money. I did not want money from her, had never looked to her as a potential source, in no way ever intended to be a burden on her, though she has very comfortable circumstances. The small amount of money meant little one way or the other... but the fact that she had wanted to send it, reduced me to tears. As I was reminded of this, I realized this is probably something that others face in one way or another. I have a better source, though... a very wealthy Father who has promised to supply

all my needs according to His riches!

As I was reading this list of "don'ts" to a friend's husband yesterday, he stopped me on "Don't write them off" and said, "That's what I did to a friend in college. I went to Bob Jones University and my best friend got in minor trouble. They told him if he wouldn't apologize they'd throw him out. He wouldn't and they did. I remember saying to him, 'If you won't do what they tell you, you realize we can no longer be friends.' He left school and I lost my best friend. I've felt guilty about what I did as a legalistic youth and I've tried to find words to say I'm sorry, but we've never gotten together. Keep telling people: Don't write them off."

How many well-meaning Christians have written someone off in a moment of poor judgment and lived to regret it. How many grandmothers can't enjoy their grandchildren because they "wrote off" their daughter for some grievous sin and have never been willing to humble themselves and restore fellowship. Oh dear friends, don't lash out with words you'll have to eat later and if you already have, eat them quickly and restore "...the years that the locusts hath eaten..." (Joel 2:25).

Don't say, "It could be worse": Somehow we feel if we can point out how much worse the circumstances could be, we'll make the person happy. When my mother had a third of her foot cut off because of a malignant tumor, I wasn't cheered by the lady who said, "Just look at it this way, they could have chopped off the whole thing." A young girl gave birth to twins. One of them died at one week old and she wrote me, "The thing I was told the most was, 'Well, at least you've got the other.' " The grieving for a dead child is not eliminated because there is an "other one."

When my daughter Lauren lost a child prematurely, some "cheered her up" by saying, "But think how lucky you are to have little Randy," or "Don't be upset, you can always have another one."

We often try to tell the afflicted about people who are worse off so they will feel better but that rarely helps. Whatever the pain of the grieving person it is maximum to them at that moment.

Don't say, "Pray about it" or "Forget it": To the person in a severe trauma the saintly words, "Pray about it," are of little comfort. We all know we should pray about our problems and work through them but there are times when some outside counsel is needed and when "forgetting about it" is not yet possible. A lovely lady I know had been attacked and molested. She had been defenseless and suffered severe emotional consequences. Her church friends told her to "Pray about it and forget it," and quoted Scripture to her. She became severely depressed and when she finally went to a Christian psychologist, the other women said she was "blaspheming the Holy Spirit" by not trusting in God. They had judged her as a heretic because she sought help in overcoming a problem they had never experienced. Don't cast off every trauma with "Pray about it and forget it." Even if you don't understand the situation or agree with the treatment, be supportive of the individual.

Don't add guilt or search for blame: It is so natural for us to want to step on one who is already down and point out more clearly how he or she got into this situation and whose fault it really is. In divorce problems it becomes almost a Monopoly game of who should advance to "Park Place" and who should "go directly to jail and do not collect $200." One lady described her pastor's concern for her in her impending divorce but explained he really had to take her husband's side because "He's one of our biggest contributors." Another woman whose Christian husband had driven off in his new Corvette with a pretty young girl was stripped of her very popular Sunday school class she had taught for twenty years. The pastor's words, "Obvious failures should not be allowed in leadership positions." A divorcee who was working hard to pull her life together and support her children went to a women's church meeting. The pastor's wife said, "There are two kinds of women here today. You who are married and you young ones who will be someday." Her message focused on these two types and those who were divorced or widowed felt ostracized. This lady said, "We are considered nonpersons in a subchurch."

I've never met a divorced person who is proud of it or who found it an exhilarating experience. None of us want it or recommend it, but when it is an accomplished fact, our Christian duty is to relieve the afflicted not heap guilt on them or show them where they were to blame.

When our families found out our first son was brain-damaged, there was a quick inspection of each side to see if there had been problems like this in the past. Somehow it seemed important to pin blame on the opposite side, but it didn't help me much to be questioned about any ancestors who might have been "a little off." At that time I was asked by several relatives if I'd left the baby on the counter and he'd fallen off, and it was inferred that my "galavanting around and leaving him with sitters" was how he was brain-damaged.

Somehow the more spiritual we think we are, the more we have need to make pronouncements that will indict others. My friend Marilyn recently got a call with the shocking news that her teenage son was in the hospital, the victim of a head-on collision caused by a drunk driver. She and her husband rushed to the hospital where the boy was in a coma. They prayed fervently and gave Nathan to the Lord for His will to be done. Nathan died. Later a consoling friend said, "Your whole problem was giving him up to the Lord and not fighting for him. If you'd kept praying and believing, he could have lived." Even if one believed what he was saying, surely nothing could be gained by telling a grieving parent the fault was theirs. How pathetic that Christians who should give comfort so often feel it's God's appointment to heap guilt on the one in need. When you are the victim of one of life's calamities, you don't need pious platitudes placing blame. Comfort, don't convict.

Don't ignore the problem: The easiest reaction to trauma in others is to ignore it. That way you don't have to view something difficult to look at or get yourself involved in something difficult to handle. In our crisis times more people choose the "ignore the problem" method than any other. If you look the other way, it may go away. And it may, but not because of you. I have talked to so many women who in times of trauma were virtually abandoned by their friends and church. No one wants to see the retarded child, no one wants to get involved in the divorce, no one knows what to do with a rape victim, and no one enjoys weepy widows or dying cancer patients. It's so much easier to look the other way. How do you feel when you're the victim? Like you've got leprosy? Like you've been abandoned? The traumas of life aren't popular. New babies and broken legs we can handle, but keep us from having to love the unlovable. Dr. John MacDonald writes in his book, *When Cancer Strikes*, that "avoidance" is one of the hardest things to take. He relates that when he had a heart operation he had many visits and cards but when he had cancer few came. He was dropped from the medical community and one day when he was feeling well enough to go out, he met a doctor friend who cried out, "My God, it's you. I thought you were dead."

If you wish to be ABOVE AVERAGE, relieve the afflicted, don't ignore them or their problems. Dr. MacDonald says, "Often the patient welcomes talking about his situation. He loathes talking around it, listening to people who pretend it's not there."[1]

Don't say, "Don't cry...": Since we don't know what to do with people who cry we instinctively tell them not to. Crying is weakness. Be strong. I was strong through the painful illnesses of my sons. I kept quiet about it. I didn't cry. Many friends never even knew of my problems. I was brave. But oh, how much grief I suppressed.

In the last two years as Marilyn Murray has spoken to C.L.A.S.S. about her therapy, which brought out many suppressed traumas of her past, she demonstrates with bottles what happens when we suppress our pain. She shows a bottle full of fluid with the cork pushed down in and says this represents many of us who have stuffed the hurts and pain under wraps. What happens when the bottle is left in a hot place? It explodes. This is what happens to many of us who have been taught to hold it all in—when things get hot, we explode. It may be a momentary flare up, a nervous breakdown or suicide. As I heard her lesson I decided to write down happenings in my life where I'd shoved the problem under the rug or at least had not dealt with my feelings openly. Without much trouble I had quite a list. How about you? If you found yourself in a hot place would your bottle explode?

Don't tell people to be brave and not to cry. Sometimes the best thing you can do for a person is hold them and let them cry. When Betty Rollins, wrote her book on her mastectomy, she titled it, *First You Cry.* I'm not suggesting that we all sit around and weep and wail forever, but do realize that crying is a release from all we bottle up inside and remember, ". . . Weeping may endure for a night, but joy cometh in the morning" (Psalm 30:5).

Why do we find it so difficult to relieve the afflicted? Ask yourself that question? Dr. MacDonald says its a reflection of our own fear of disease or problems, and it's because we don't know what to say or are unable to handle emotional problems. Many of us have not dealt with our *own* emotional problems and therefore are ill-equipped to uplift others. Many of us naturally turn from troubles and some say, "I've got enough of my own." Some don't want to be associated with anyone who's "not with it" now or seen with someone who's on the wrong side of a divorce.

It's a lot easier to ignore problems than deal with them, to condemn rather than understand. But if we want to be ABOVE AVERAGE, what can we do?

It Takes So Little To Be ABOVE AVERAGE.

27

Comfort Ye My People

Comfort ye, comfort ye my people, saith your God.
Isaiah 40:1

To comfort is to "cheer in time of grief or trouble, to relieve pain." God has instructed us to cheer his people in time of trouble and yet it is so difficult to do. One lady excused herself by saying, "It's just not my gift." It's not mine either. I'm so poor at dealing with sickness that my family says I have a "lack of nurseness." But God did not say, "Comfort ye my people," if you have a feel for it, if it's your gift, if it's convenient. In Psalm 69:20 is a plaintive verse: "I looked for some[one] to take pity, but there was none; and for comforters but I found none." This verse describes some of those in our Christian community. People with buckets of burdens looking for people with armloads of answers but finding few real comforters, few who are ready to give cheer in time of grief. This lack of desire to help is especially noticed in the areas of "unpopular problems" such as rape, incest, and child molestation.

Two years ago I thought those troubles were either fiction or far away. I had read the accepted figure that one out of four girls by the age of sixteen is the victim of some form of sexual molestation, but I didn't know any of them. The first time Marilyn Murray spoke on this subject during C.L.A.S.S. at the Crystal

Cathedral, I was dumbfounded when out of a group of eighty ABOVE AVERAGE women, twenty-five came to Marilyn and poured out their traumas. In San Antonio out of one hundred eighty women, sixty identified themselves as victims and in Walnut Creek thirty-five out of one hundred ten.

Suddenly I had to face the fact that good Christian women have had the same proportion of sexual molestation as the national average. Marilyn had to stay extra days in each city to "comfort my people." As she listened to them, the majority started by saying, "I've never told this to anyone before." Why? Because they *knew* no one would ever understand. As Marilyn shared about her experience, she had pushed buttons on women who had been waiting to find someone who would understand, who could comfort them in their hidden grief. All had suppressed their feelings and those few who had sought Christian counsel had been told to pray about it and forget it. Some had been instructed to never mention this to anyone again, some were told that rape victims ask for it, and some that "I'm sure it's all in your head." None of these answers is a comfort to one whose bottle is about to explode.

While lay people are not equipped to counsel trauma victims, we can at least be sensitive to the desperate needs around us and realize there are many heavy hearts with hidden burdens.

God wants us to have our eyes open, to comfort his people, to relieve the afflicted. ABOVE AVERAGE women are all in demand. Isaiah 50:4 says, "The Lord God hath given me the tongue of the learned, that I should know how to speak a word in season to him that is weary...." What can we do to comfort the depressed, the defenseless, the diseased, the dying?

Try to understand: Even though we may never have been through the causal experience of the distressed person, we can try to understand. We can tell them of some similar feeling we've had even if from a different set of circumstances. Almost everyone who is distraught thinks at that moment that no one understands. People relate best to someone who's been there. Because I've had marriage problems, lost two brain-damaged sons, and experienced depression, women know I'll understand in these areas. Because Marilyn was the victim of a sexual attack as a child, women see for the first time someone who will understand.

Because Barbara Bueler was the victim of a shooting and also lost her home and all her belongings in a fire, women know she will have compassion. Because Francine Jackson comes from a broken home, has experienced repeated rejections and is now rising to the challenge of stepfamily living, women flock to her for comfort.

A dear young girl named Sally approached me after I gave my testimony in Birmingham telling me about her 16-month-old baby still in the hospital from birth with multiple brain-damage problems. Sally was emotionally drained, felt she needed to get out of town, and was sure no one understood her. Later she wrote me:

> I want to express my deepest thank you for understanding and giving the advice that it wouldn't be so wrong of me to want to get away from the situation with my daughter. So many people do not understand why I would leave this baby, but I absolutely have to for my own health. I do not want to upset you by making you dwell on the situation with your two sons; you have gone through it, survived it, are a very strong woman to go on sharing it in your conferences, books, et cetera. I know how much it hurts to tell others about this type thing. Just think of it like this—you are reaching out to people who have sick kids like me. You have helped me already. May God give you as much strength as you need to go on sharing with others.

The most constant statement I hear in marriage counseling is, "He doesn't understand." This statement means he "doesn't comprehend the nature or the character" of the person or the problem. If we can only try to understand, we will comfort the people.

Listen: Once people think we understand or at least want to understand, they will pour out their problems and all we have to do is listen. We don't have to be brilliant or even have a three-step solution, we only have to listen. No one listens to anyone any more; they're all too busy, so if we just listen we become a devoted friend. Everywhere I go, on planes, in lines, in the ladies room, I find people who give me their buckets of burdens. I don't have to make up case histories, I only have to listen. They can sense that I care and they talk. Sometimes a stranger after pouring out a whole life upon me will suddenly say, "I don't know why I told you all this." She had to tell it to someone and I was there.

My dear friend Frances Thomas in Dallas has been coping with cancer for many years. When I asked her how people could be of help to her she replied:

> The key to the whole thing is to LISTEN. Some days we want to talk about it and some days we don't, so be sensitive.

Frances, who says her aim in life is "to be attuned to what God wants me to do for Him," says her "greatest asset is the love of godly friends."

Be available to listen. Long-term patients especially need to have someone sit beside them. Dr. MacDonald says they don't fear death so much as they fear being alone.

Sometimes our greatest ministry to one in bereavement or one waiting through a loved one's surgery is to just be there and be sensitive. The poet John Milton said, "They also serve who only stand and wait."[1]

Do Something Specific: When we try to understand others' problems and are willing to listen, we help the hurting hearts. Now what can we do for them physically?

Obviously each problem has different needs but let's look at some practical solutions. Average people often say, "If there's anything I can do, let me know." ABOVE AVERAGE people do something specific.

At the time of a death, **drop in** to express your love, **call** to let them know you care, or **visit** the funeral home. **Send flowers,** a memorial **gift,** or a **card.** Always add a **personal note** expressing some warm thoughts about the deceased.

Tana Reiff, in an article in *McCall's* magazine, writes:

> Of the many personal visits and cards and letters my mother received at the time of my father's death, she says, "I was particularly comforted by those that recalled a special memory of how my husband's life in-

fluenced theirs. It was wonderful to hear for the first time stories about things he had done years ago."[2]

Elizabeth Swank, who attended the Ft. Worth C.L.A.S.S., wrote:

My husband, after fifty years in the ministry (forty-three as pastor of one church) died suddenly last fall. I received hundreds of cards, letters, expressing sympathy. I soon saw that most fell into one of two categories. One was the "devotional thought" with Scripture—pointing to the joys of heaven, etc. The second which I found much more comforting were the "I-will-miss-him-too" expressions which included some humorous story or some generous act involving my husband. They mostly ended with "I'm so glad I knew him." Certainly, I'll remember this when I try to comfort others.

If you **bring food** to a family this gesture is always appreciated whether it is because of a death, a hospital stay, sickness at home or just some bad news. Putting the effort into cooking something yourself always has an uplifting effect. Last winter when I had a brief bout with pneumonia, Lynn Hall, a young mother in our church, called to say she heard I was sick and she was bringing me dinner. It was the first time in years that anyone had done this for me and I was excitedly shocked. I'll never forget that catered dinner and that dear girl who cared enough to prepare it.

When I was visiting the home of Joann and Mel Turner in Dallas, they had a friend whose husband was in the hospital. The friend had been down there constantly and had not been able to keep her house in order. I was amazed when Joann had her own cleaning lady accompany her to **clean the friend's house.** At dinner that night Joann said there had been so much to do that both of them had worked on the house all day. To me that kind of service for a friend is ABOVE AVERAGE.

When my babies were ill and I had been told there was no hope, I didn't care if I lived another day. Going to one more doctor to get the same answers was sometimes more than I thought I could handle. During that period I had one friend who **called every morning** at 9 A.M. Louise Knaut checked in to see if I had any needs that day and if I did she filled them. She **ran errands** and **picked my girls up** at school, but most of all she **went with me** to my doctor appointments. She never put any pressure on me and although she was a very busy woman, she sat patiently with me in many waiting rooms. That's an ABOVE AVERAGE friend!

When Jan Crafton at Ft. Worth was going through an unwanted divorce, much of the Christian community looked the other way. I asked her if there had been one person who had been helpful and she answered:

> At the top of the list must be my precious friend who is closer than a sister to me. She just **stood by me**, and came to be with me at any hour of the day or the night, and no matter how impossible I was, no matter if I cried or got angry, no matter what, she just hung in there and never took offense, and kept on loving me, and kept on enduring the pain with me...talk about un- conditional love! That same friend literally took me by the hand, and **led me back to my Bible**, which I had lost the habit of reading. She just said, in desperation, not knowing what else to do with me, "Come on, Jan, let's read." And those words just leaped off the page at me, they just began to nourish and strengthen me like cool water to a starving person. I had read the Bible all my life, and I didn't know how wonderful it was until then.

Wendy Bergren of Walnut Creek is a young mother struggling to beat cancer. Many people have volunteered to help and from her lengthy illness she compiled what had been the most mean- ingful to her. She wrote twenty suggestions including:

> Cook a dinner and bring it in disposable containers.
> Bake cookies and bring them frozen.
> Offer to babysit.
> Wrap presents for my children to take to parties.
> Take snapshots of my children.
> Encourage your husband to visit mine.

You are all creative people and you can custom-make your

kindnesses to fit the needs of the people.

Follow through: Don't tell anyone you will do something and then not do it. Idle words such as, "I'll call you in a few weeks," may be the hope a person clings to that is shattered when you in your busy life forget to call. Some say they have a "great book" that will help, and then don't bring it. Some say, "You will love my apple pie," and don't bake one. The average person means well, but it takes someone ABOVE AVERAGE to follow through.

Hug and touch: Many times we are afraid we won't know what to say at a funeral and so we don't go or we sneak out. At that point the family doesn't want a fascinating monologue; they just want to know you cared enough to come. A touch on the hand or an arm around the shoulders is far more helpful than a few clever sentences about how impressed you are with the hearse.

Cancer victims especially need to be hugged or patted since many receive vibrations from friends that they are contagious. Those of us with retarded or abnormal children want a friend who will hold that child instead of turn from him. Some people can't and we understand, but we will love the friend who will love our child.

Continue to include: The hardest thing to bear for a person who has lost a mate through death or divorce is that their friends frequently drop them from the social roster. Since they no longer fit the norm, they are left out. It takes an ABOVE AVERAGE person to care enough to be creative and include the single friend.

Hold confidences: You wouldn't think this point would need to be made in Christian circles but I hear so frequently of a person who poured her heart out at a moment of trauma only to hear it all back a few weeks later from a different source. I've known pastors who have told their wives, who have told their prayer group, who have told their friends. When a person is already distraught and has shared confidences they've never told a soul before, they fall apart when they find their life on the prayer chain.

Share Scripture: At the moment of crisis most people don't want a saintly friend reminding them that "all things work together for good to those who love the Lord and are called according to his purpose." Twenty years down the line I can see that God has taken the tragedies of my life and used them to bring me to my knees and to the Savior, but I wouldn't have enjoyed hearing it back then. Whatever the problem, be sensitive to when you should share a Scripture with the needy friend. Some want words of hope immediately and others, who have decided for the moment that there is no God, will be angered or turned off. God is not pushy and He will give you direction at the right time.

Love and accept: Even though we all preach unconditional love, we have trouble really living it. We get along fine with those who agree with us and live according to our standards but it's difficult not to judge the sinner and condemn the fallen. If we know more than ten verses by heart we feel called upon to stand with Moses and discern with Solomon. We tend to say, "I love you if..." and "I'll accept you when...."

What was Jesus' attitude toward the person caught up in moral problems? In John 8:1-11 we read a simple story. Jesus is teaching a Bible study. He has no doubt worked on it all week and has passed out the study guides. He has everyone's attention focused on the heart of his message when the real spiritual giants who know everything walk in. They haven't had time for learning from the Lord because they are the "Secret Spirit Squad" sent out to spy. They try to turn up a few sinners a day to help purify the church. Today they have a biggie—a woman caught in adultery "in the very act." They know Jesus would want this important information even though he's in the middle of teaching, so they barge right in and set her in the midst of the group. In case Jesus has forgotten the rules, they remind him such a sinner should be stoned to death.

But Jesus doesn't overreact. Instead he looks at this legalistic lot and says, "He that is without sin among you, let him first cast a stone at her." Can you imagine the soul-searching that went on at that time? As they each listen to the drip, drip, drip of their conscience, one by one they drop away. Jesus has his head down; he doesn't care to check who leaves in what order. When they are all gone, he looks up and asks the woman where her accusers are. He doesn't give her a lecture; he doesn't recite the Ten Commandments.

Can you imagine what we might be led to do at such a moment faced with a proven sinner caught in the very act? Could we resist a few condemning verses? Wouldn't we lead her in the Sinner's Prayer? Would we carry her to a confession booth, call the church elders, or capture the moment on film? Would we pull her down to the sand and have her kneel over a rock of repentance?

You can be sure we would have made an example of her if not an exhibit. But what did Jesus do? He quietly asked, "Hath no man condemned thee?"

She answered, "No man, Lord." And Jesus said to her, "Neither do I condemn thee: go and sin no more."

Jesus loved her and accepted her as she was. He didn't preach, judge or say, "If you were really a Christian, you wouldn't have done this." He didn't blame it on the devil or tell horror stories of what happened to others caught in adultery. He forgave her and he comforted his people. Jesus was and is and ever more will be an ABOVE AVERAGE man. How about you and me?

It Takes So Little To Be ABOVE AVERAGE.

9

It Takes So Little
To Pray Above Average

28

Coming Home to Prayer

Do you pray ABOVE AVERAGE? If average includes everyone in the world, then if you prayed at all, you pray ABOVE AVERAGE. But how can you do better? As Barbara Bueler learned, when she gave the simple prayer outline for ladies to write inside their Bibles, there is an interest in prayer and few feel they know how to do it. When Nina Jean Obel mentions the material she wrote on how to pray, women rush to get copies.

Why is there a renewed interest in prayer? The reason is because all else has failed. In this country we have believed in ourselves and our ability to rise from nothing to greatness. We started as an odd collection of pilgrims seeking religious freedom and fugitives from the law of other countries. Like a child who has run away from home, we wanted to show our Father we could make it on our own. With many struggles we grew up and we became the greatest. The United States of America has been on top with its form of government, its military, its resources, its education, its morals, its families, its individuals. When you're the best, you don't need outside help.

What has happened, however, in the last ten years? Our government has been hurt by scandal, our cities are unmanageable and on the verge of bankruptcy, our leaders fear for their lives.

Our military is no longer the super power we once believed it was, being in the service does not bear the patriotic fervor it once did, and we fear the threat of nuclear war from a force far superior to ours.

Our resources are not sufficient for our needs. Our economy has been manipulated by outside influences and many of our manufactured products are not competitive on the world market.

Our education is at its worst point in history. As I quoted earlier, the Commission on Excellence found only "pockets of excellence" to praise, and reported the current school population to be the first generation in our history to know less than its parents.

Our moral fibers have been frazzled. As a nation we have abandoned any semblance of moral standards. We've grown up, we're out on our own; we don't have to live by Father's house rules any more. In this time of sexual freedom, we have seen more mental breakdowns and emotional traumas than ever before. As one headline lamented, "There's no freedom in the free lifestyle." In my seminars filled with outstanding Christian women, we find victims of rape, incest, and molestation; we find mothers of drug abusers, homosexuals, runaways, and cultists; we find wives of abusive men, adulterers, and alcoholics.

Our families are falling apart and the Christian world is no exception. At Lover's Lane Methodist in Dallas the adult class for singles over thirty-five years old numbers more than six hundred participants! They have an effective ministry and one that is desperately needed. Infidelity is now so acceptable we're hardly shocked and the ease of divorce has made marriage commitment a temporary condition.

So that brings me down to ME and I'm not even sure of ME. I'm lonely, insecure and fearful. Where can ME turn for help?

As a country we grew up to greatness; we got fat and rich. We ran away from restrictions, plunged into pleasure, and sought self-gratification. Now like the prodigal son, we've run the gamut and we want to come home. We're finally desperate enough to admit we've made mistakes and to confess them to our Father.

Will He forgive us? Will He take us back? Does He hear us knocking at the gate?

> When he was yet a great way off, his father saw him,
> and had compassion and ran, and fell on his neck and
> kissed him.
>
> Luke 15:20

When all else fails, we can come home:

> And it shall come to pass that before they call, I will
> answer; and while they are yet speaking, I will hear.
> Isaiah 65:24

Before you call, your Father hears you. The prodigal son confessed his sins and his father had an instant celebration. He didn't give him a lecture at the gate or say, "I told you so." He brought out the best robe, put a ring on his hand and shoes on his feet. He killed the fatted calf; they ate and were merry because what was lost had been found.

Have you run away from home? Have you gone to the end of the road? Has the world and its pleasures failed you? Are you ready to come home to your Father?

How do you pray ABOVE AVERAGE? You remember the prodigal son who had "wasted his substance on riotous living" and then "came to himself" and turned home. He didn't bring a big list of requests, he just came to the gate with a humble and contrite heart.

How about you? Have you been praying below average prayers? Have you been asking for favors, presenting conditions or calling for help when you're still in the far country? Come home. Come home!

> Draw nigh to God and He will draw nigh to you.
> James 4:8

★   ★   ★

COME HOME: Dear Father, I've come home.

Here's where I've been: _____

_____

_____

_____

_____

_____

Here's what I've been doing: _____

_____

_____

_____

_____

_____

Here's the trouble I've gotten into: _____

_____

_____

_____

_____

_____

I know You are always "nigh unto them that are of a broken heart" (Psalm 34:18).

I know You are a "God at hand...and not a God afar off" and I'm home (Jeremiah 23:23).

CALL OUT: Dear Lord, I know You are standing and knocking at the door of my heart. I want You to come in and sup with me. The world has failed me. I'm alone. You've told me in the past, "Call to me, and I will answer you, and I will show you great and mighty things which you do not know." Father, I don't know much. Tell me great and mighty things. I'm willing to listen. "I cried unto the Lord with my voice...." (Psalm 142:1). I'm waiting for Your reply.

CONFESS: Dear Father,

I've wasted much of my life in: _____

_____

_____

_____

I've said unkind things to:_____

_____

_____

I need to forgive: _____

_____

_____

You've told me if I confess my sins You are faithful and just to forgive me and to cleanse me from all unrighteousness (I John 1:9).

I confess: _____

_____

_____

CELEBRATE: Dear Father, I've *come home*, I've *called out*. I've *confessed*. Bring me into Your home and let's *celebrate* together. I feel Your warmth and Your welcome. "Let my prayer be set forth before thee as incense...." (Psalm 141:2). As we sit at Your table and eat the fatted calf, I see Jesus Christ at Your right hand, making intercession for me (Romans 8:34). While I've been away, He's been there beside You putting in a good word for me. Let's celebrate, for he who was lost has returned.

Thank You for Your mantle which You've placed over my shoulders that I might never be cold again. Thank You for the ring of love You've placed on my finger that I may reach out a caring hand and relieve the afflicted. Thank You for the shoes on my feet that I might walk in Your path and spread Your words wherever I go.

Dear Father:

      I've **COME HOME**
      I've **CALLED OUT**
      I've **CONFESSED**, now
      Let's **CELEBRATE** in Jesus' precious name,
                 AMEN.

What a Father we have:

> Above Heaven and Earth
> Above every living creature
> ABOVE AVERAGE!

Because of who *He* is:

> *It Takes So Little To Be ABOVE AVERAGE.*

BIBLIOGRAPHY

Chapter 1

1. *Newsweek*, August 6, 1979.
2. Cook, op cit., introduction.
3. Proverbs 31:10.
4. *Time*, June 20, 1983.

Chapter 2

1. *Los Angeles Times*, November 30, 1980.
2. *Los Angeles Times*, July 20, 1982.
3. Ibid.
4. Matthew 7:13-14.

Chapter 3

1. David A. Seamans, *Healing for Damaged Emotions*, (Wheaton: Victor Books), 1981.

Chapter 4

1. *Los Angeles Times*, March 31, 1983.

Chapter 8

1. Shakespeare's *Julius Caesar*, Act I, Scene 2.
2. *Newsweek*, May 9, 1983, "Can the Schools Be Saved?"
3. *Newsweek,* December 14, 1981, "Thinking: A Neglected Art."
4. *Newsweek*, May 9, 1983, op cit.
5. *Newsweek*, December 14, 1981, op cit.

Chapter 9

1. *Newsweek*, May 9, 1983, op cit.
2. *Los Angeles Times*, May 18, 1983.
3. *Newsweek*, April 19, 1982.
4. *Newsweek*, February 7, 1983.
5. Ibid.
6. *Forbes,* December 20, 1982, "How to Think Sideways."
7. *Time,* June 20, 1983.

Chapter 10

1. *Forbes,* December 20, 1982, op cit.
2. Philippians 2:5.

Chapter 12

1. David K. Lindo, "Thank God It's Monday," *The Toastmaster*, December, 1982.
2. *Los Angeles Times,* September 15, 1981.

Chapter 13

1. Dorrine Anderson Turecamo, "The World...According to Your Journal," *The Toastmaster,*November, 1982.
2. Robert W. Johnston, "Whole Mind Power," *The Toastmaster,* December, 1982.
3. Jerry Mason, "A Different Way to Pray," *Discipleship Journal,* Issue Fifteen, 1983.
4. Sharon Sexton, "Diaries Open New Pages To Ourselves," *USA Today,* April 28, 1983.
5. Ibid.
6. 1 Samuel 16:1 (NIV).

Chapter 14

1. Proverbs 15:1.
2. John 12:32.

Chapter 15

1. *United,* June, 1983.
2. *Time,* February 8, 1983.
3. Ibid.
4. Ibid.
5. Ibid.

Chapter 16

1. *Forbes,* December 20, 1982, op. cit.

2. Ibid.

Chapter 17

1. *Times,* June 20, 1983.
2. Ibid.

Chapter 22

1. Jim Newman, *Release Your Brakes,* New York: Warner Books).

Chapter 23

1. *Reader's Digest Dictionary.*

Chapter 26

1. John A. Mac Donald, M.D., *When Cancer Strikes,* (Spectrum Publishers), Chapter 2.

Chapter 27

1. John Milton, *On His Blindness.*
2. Tana Reiff, "If There's Anything I Can Do...,"*McCall's,* February, 1983.

Dear Reader,

If you have been challenged by this book and feel more should be written on any one of these areas, please let me know. If, for example, you have been through any of the traumas mentioned in the chapters titled, "Relieve the Afflicted" or "Comfort Ye My People" and would be willing to share an example, we would appreciate your contribution. If you wish to write:

- Describe the problem situation
- Tell what people did to help
- Tell what people did that hurt
- . Explain the results
- Give practical suggestions

If you wish to have a Christian Leaders and Speakers Seminar (C.L.A.S.S.) in your area or to engage any of the C.L.A.S.S. speakers for your church, please write to:

> Fred Littauer
> C.L.A.S.S.
> 1666 E. Highland Avenue
> San Bernardino, CA 92404

For further information on Florence Littauer's C.L.A.S.S. tape album, please send the attached card to:

> HARVEST HOUSE PUBLISHERS
> 1075 Arrowsmith
> Eugene, OR 97402